# John
## THE BAPTIST
### *Prophet and Disciple*

**ALEXANDER J. BURKE, JR.**

## ST. ANTHONY MESSENGER PRESS
Cincinnati, Ohio

Scripture passages have been taken from *New Revised Standard Version Bible*, copyright ©1989 by the Division of Christian Education of the National Council of the Churches of Christ in the U.S.A., and used by permission. All rights reserved.

Photo credits:
p. 48: Rodin, Auguste, *John the Baptist Preaching*. Photo Credit: Digital Image © The Museum of Modern Art/Licensed by SCALA / Art Resource, NY; van Rijn, Rembrandt, *The Preaching of Saint John the Baptist*. Photo Credit: Bildarchiv Preussischer Kulturbesitz / Art Resource, NY

p. 140: Grünewald, Mathias, *Crucifixion*. A panel from the Isenheim Altar. Photo Credit: Erich Lessing/ Art Resource, NY

p. 157: Frontal view of the ivory throne of Maximian. Photo Credit: Alinari / Art Resource, NY

p. 178: Angelico, Fra, *Choir of Prophets*. Photo Credit: Alinari / Art Resource, NY

p. 179: Eyck, Jan van, Ghent Altarpiece, detail of *God the Father, the Virgin Mary, John the Baptist, and Adoration of the Mystic Lamb*. Photo Credit: Scala / Art Resource, NY; Dürer, Albrecht (1471-1528), *The Adoration of the Trinity*, with Dürer's self-portrait at the bottom right. Photo Credit: Erich Lessing/Art Resource, NY

p.180: Greco, El (1541-1614), *Burial of Count Orgaz*. Photo Credit: Giraudon / Art Resource, NY; Weyden, Roger van der, *Saint John the Baptist with Resurrection of the dead*. Detail of the *Last Judgment, 1434*. Photo Credit: Erich Lessing / Art Resource, NY

Cover design by Candle Light Studios
Cover painting: Caravaggio, Michelangelo Merisi da, *Saint John the Baptist*.
Photo Credit : Nimatallah / Art Resource, NY
Book design by Mark Sullivan

LIBRARY OF CONGRESS CATALOGING-IN-PUBLICATION DATA

Burke, Alexander J.
   John the Baptist : prophet and disciple / Alexander J. Burke, Jr.
      p. cm.
   ISBN-13: 978-0-86716-737-5 (pbk. : alk. paper)
   ISBN-10: 0-86716-737-8 (pbk. : alk. paper)
   1. John, the Baptist, Saint.    I. Title.
   BS2456.B86 2006
   232.9'4—dc22
                                                        2005037097


ISBN-10: 0–86716–737–8
ISBN-13: 978–0–86716–737–5
Copyright ©2006, Alexander J. Burke, Jr. All rights reserved.

Published by St. Anthony Messenger Press
28 W. Liberty St.
Cincinnati, OH 45202
www.AmericanCatholic.org

Printed in the United States of America.

Printed on acid-free paper.

06 07 08 09 10   5 4 3 2 1

*To my extended family:*
*my wife, my seven children*
*and their spouses,*
*and my eighteen grandchildren,*
*who have all enriched my life*
*beyond measure.*

# Contents

# The Enigma of John the Baptist

John THE BAPTIST IS ONE OF THE MOST MYSTERIOUS figures in the New Testament. Part of this mystery derives from the many contradictions found in different portrayals of him—those in each of the four Gospels, in the Acts of the Apostles and in the Jewish historian Josephus's *Antiquities of the Jews.* The aim of this book is to develop a unified portrait of this complex figure, assembled clue by clue, one mosaic tile at a time.

Gabriel Marcel, the great French philosopher, drew a classic distinction between a problem and a mystery. One relates personally to a mystery—it is a subjective experience—but a problem is an objective intellectual exercise. One becomes involved intellectually and emotionally in a mystery, much as Saint Paul involves us in the mystery of Christ. John the Baptist is not a problem to be solved. He is a mystery to be plumbed and appreciated. To probe the mystery of this prophetic figure, we must recognize and then attempt to reconcile some of the many contradictory statements made about him: Some say John was a prophet, but many deny it. John himself denies he is Elijah (John 1:21), but Jesus asserts, "If you are willing to accept it, he is Elijah who is to come" (Matthew 11:14; note, however, the qualifying condition that Jesus puts on his affirmation). Jesus gives John one of the greatest compliments he ever gives to anyone, saying, "Among those born of women, no one has arisen greater than John the Baptist." Then, he immediately seems to retract it when he says, "yet the least in the kingdom of heaven is greater than he" (Matthew 11:11). Some have claimed that John was a member of the Essene community at Qumran, but others have stoutly opposed this contention. Many see John as a figure rooted solely in Second Temple Judaism—the religious culture of the time; others see him as the first saint and martyr of Christianity. Some see John's baptism as only a Judaic rite of purification or as a form of Jewish proselyte baptism; others see John's baptism as a very new rite—the prototype of Christian baptism.

What did John know about Jesus and when did he know it? In both Matthew 11:3 and Luke 7:19, John asks Jesus from his prison cell: "Are you the one who is to come or should we seek another?" suggesting that John received no divine revelation that Jesus was the Messiah. Why do some report that John the Baptist recognized Jesus in the womb (Luke 1:41, 44) and later baptized him, yet elsewhere give no indication that he had any knowledge of Jesus—his cousin—in his ministry?

Why did John baptize Jesus? There are radical differences in the accounts of this event in each of the Synoptic Gospels, and the fourth Gospel omits even any mention of the event. What can it have meant for a sinless Jesus to undergo John's baptism?

Matthew leaves us this puzzling report: "From the days of John the Baptist until now the kingdom of heaven has suffered violence, and the violent take it by force. For all the prophets and the law prophesied until John came" (Matthew 11:12–13). Can we storm the gates of heaven? Was John the cessation of the prophets and the law?

In his infancy narratives, Luke gives us a startling revelation about John even before his birth: "even before his birth he will be filled with the Holy Spirit" (1:15) and ". . . the child leaped in her womb. And Elizabeth was filled with the Holy Spirit" (1:41).

What was the role of the Holy Spirit in John's life? How was he sanctified even before his birth?

These questions offer a sampling of the issues and clues that must be assembled into a clear pattern if we are to construct a rounded view of John, as luminous as those ancient Byzantine mosaic portraits of him.

The tough questions we face help us define both the complexity of this man and the fascination he has held for so many. Let us penetrate this mystery a little deeper by listing and commenting on some other tough questions and issues.

The question should be asked: What does this book add to the literature on John the Baptist and what original contributions does it make? First, very few books for a general audience have been written on John the Baptist; none have been written in the last fifty years. The vast majority of the books on John are scholarly works on Scripture, and most of these are attempts to pursue the quest for the historical John, an effort that parallels in methodology and intent the fashionable, but limited, quest for the "historical" Jesus. These scriptural campaigns to uncover what they see as the historical vestiges within the Gospel accounts founder on the fact that the evangelists were not interested in Enlightenment concepts of scientific history but in proclaiming the message of salvation. Such books suffer from a fixation on history that leads them to see John solely as a figure of Second Temple Judaism—merely a product of his culture. They miss most of the factors that have made John significant in Christian history. Why did each of the four evangelists make John the gateway to the Gospel, the first preacher of the good news? What were the reasons for the early church's intense interest in a desert hermit whose public ministry lasted two years or less? Why in early Christian tradition was John the Baptist accorded an exalted religious stature, almost equal to that of Mary? The irony is that most modern scholarship on John has missed the true sources of his religious significance because these lie not in his ties to Second Temple Judaism, but in his links to Christ and to the very beginnings of the Christian religion.

4

Before we address the major themes of this portrait of John, it will be useful to understand the reasons for the comparative neglect of John the Baptist in modern Christian tradition versus the prominence he was accorded in early Christian tradition from A.D. 60 to 1600.

John's emphasis in his preaching was on sin, repentance, judgment and hell—topics that run counter to the more user-friendly religion of the twenty-first century. Karl Menninger in his 1974 book *Whatever Became of Sin?* notes that the very word *sin* has disappeared from our vocabulary, and any sense of guilt that would lead to repentance is, for modern psychology, morbid and a sign of a sickness of the spirit. A modern agenda has replaced John's; it repudiates the seven deadly sins as quaint and puritanical and, thus, suggests that they have disappeared.

Members of the Jesus Seminar school have been eager to promote a Jesus whose concern was for the here and now. Thus, they downplay the role of John the Baptist with his apocalyptic focus on the last things, and on a God with the winnowing fork in his hand, who is burning the chaff with unquenchable fire (see Matthew 3:12).

John's view of the end of the world, his eschatology, saw a world about to be destroyed by God in an imminent fiery judgment. Such images are so distasteful to the modern mind that we reject them out of hand. But it is useful to be reminded of the yawning religious and cultural gap that separates the historical John and Jesus of the first century from modern Americans.

John's message of justice and judgment (as in his criticism of Herod Antipas and his wife) is harsher than Jesus' message of mercy and love, though each point of John's message finds its correlative in the words of Jesus.

When we weigh these factors, we understand better why John's call—to all Israel in his time and to all human beings of our time—for a transformation of mind, heart and conduct has not been heeded.

A new book on John the Baptist needs to find its emphasis in John's role as the first Christian and in his position in world history. We need to rediscover not the historical John, but the man who was the last of the prophets and the first of the Christians. It is John's unique position in world history that is the basis of his significance. Like the ancient Colossus of Rhodes that spanned that harbor, John bridges together the Old Testament and the New Testament with a foot in each camp. Yes, his roots were in Second Temple Judaism, but his significance is in first-century Christianity. He is himself the dividing point of the ages, the living boundary marker for the new dispensation, the proclaimer of the fullness of time. What is unique about John is not what is old or rooted in the past, but what is new and rooted in the future.

John's emergence from the Palestinian desert after twenty years of life as a hermit was a startling event to the Jews of his day. He appeared as the last of the prophets and as a fulfillment of the prophecies of Isaiah (40:3) and Malachi (3:1; 4:5). We will look in detail later at these prophecies, but John's voice crying out in the wilderness was the first true prophetic voice to be heard in Israel after a silence of 450 years!

A basic theme of the whole New Testament is summarized by God from his throne in Revelation 21:5: "See, I am making all things new!" John the Baptist establishes in himself a new tradition of desert spirituality. He preaches a new message of repentance, fasting and prayer. Even before Christ, he abandons substantially the foundations of the Hebrew religion—the Temple and the Torah—and brings a totally new form of administered baptism. As the forerunner of Christ, he prepares both for the coming of Christ and for his own demise. "He must increase, but I must decrease" (John 3:30). Each of the evangelists saw John's role as so crucial that each makes John the gateway to his Gospel.

In addition, John is referred to in the New Testament more than ninety times, more than any other figure except Jesus, Peter and Paul. As the baptizer of Christ, John became the first witness of the Trinity, a role that has perpetuated his memory in Christian tradition. John the Baptist was priest, prophet and servant, just as Christ was priest, prophet and king. No one else in the Gospels stands out as serving in those three crucial roles.

The New Testament is a different kind of book. It is not primarily a work of history, though it uses history. It is not a work of information, though it imparts a wealth of information. It is, above all, a work of transformation. It aims to change the lives of its readers. And in so doing, it is a work of proclamation (kerygma), part doctrine, part biography, part narrative, part history. And we must look at how John contributes to each of these aspects.

It is the paradox of John the Baptist that he is at once both the forerunner and the follower of Christ. To understand his contribution in these two critical roles, we need to move beyond the different portrayals of John in the Gospels to his role in Christian history. So the movement of this book will proceed from Scripture to history to art to spirituality. We cannot look only at John's role in the New Testament because his significance is revealed also in his impact on Christian art, Christian theology and Christian monastic traditions and spirituality.

Thus, this book will be part biography, part history, part biblical exegesis, part spirituality and part artistic illumination. It will not be a work of biblical scholarship, though it will be informed by biblical scholarship, as well as by later Christian history. This book aims at placing John the Baptist in a historical perspective of his own times and ours in exploring his example and meaning for Christian spirituality today. A goal of this portrait is to correct the distorted picture of John found in the work of historical critics who see John only as a figure of Second Temple Judaism. We will draw on many sources beyond the Gospels, Acts and Josephus. We shall draw on the testimony of such witnesses as Christian history, monasticism, art and spirituality. We shall also call to the witness stand many of the early church fathers as well as a number of later doctors and scholars.

If we can penetrate deep into the mystery of this enigmatic figure, we may take a step toward restoring John to the place of honor he enjoyed in early Christianity among the greatest Christian heroes and martyrs.

A word on the method of presentation used in this book will help the reader to understand its goals. We do a close analysis of scriptural passages that deal with John the Baptist, informed by biblical scholarship. It is a literary and critical analysis of Scripture in context. We employ the ancient and well-established principle of interpreting Scripture by Scripture. Therefore, we compare Gospels to one another, while observing the integrity of each Gospel. We use other passages to illuminate the passages under scrutiny.

Our point of view is directly counter to one now prevalent in studies of John the Baptist that see him exclusively as an Old Testament figure who looks only backward to the past. We see John's significance as the sole biblical figure who straddles the Old Testament and the New Testament, who is the boundary marker of the ages, who is both a prophet of and a participant in the new eschatological age, and whose role as both forerunner and follower of Christ accounts for his high reputation in later Christianity, an exalted reputation exceeded only by Mary. By looking at John's later reputation in Christian history and art, we bring to bear the perspective of the ages to an assessment of John, a perspective that will show how the perspective of the historical critical biblical scholars is perhaps too finely focused. John was the first to reveal God's plan for the ages, a role that as the first letter of Peter tells us most of the prophets and even the angels could only long to share:

> Concerning this salvation, the prophets who prophesied of the grace that was to be yours made careful search and inquiry, inquiring about the person or time that the Spirit of Christ within them indicated, when it testified in advance to the sufferings destined for Christ and the subsequent glory. It was

revealed to them that they were serving not themselves but you, in regard to the things that have now been announced to you through those who brought you good news by the Holy Spirit sent from heaven—things into which angels long to look! (1 Peter 1:10–12)

## QUESTIONS FOR REFLECTION

- How can John the Baptist—that fiery preacher of sin and repentance, of justice and judgment—regain his ancient popularity in a modern world that seeks only a user-friendly religion?
- What does it mean to view John the Baptist as the boundary marker for the new dispensation?
- As you begin this exploration of the life and ministry of John the Baptist, what meaning do you give to the abiding images of John as Baptist, as forerunner, as witness, as prophet?

# CHAPTER ONE

# The Birth of John and the Birth of Jesus: The Parallel Accounts

It IS IN SOME WAYS SURPRISING THAT WE HAVE ANY ACCOUNT at all of the birth of John the Baptist. Two of the Gospels, Mark and John, have no account even of the birth of Jesus. Matthew has an account of the birth of Jesus, but not of John. Only Luke presents an account of the birth of John, and his version is governed by two literary principles: First, he makes the account of John's birth a direct and detailed parallel to the birth of Jesus; second, he writes his account of both births in the tradition of the births of Old Testament prophets and of classical biographies of heroic figures. Luke is the most accomplished New Testament writer. He writes also, as his prologues to his Gospel and to his Acts of the Apostles testify, in the tradition of classical writers of history, and he writes the most elegant Greek in all of the New Testament, excepting perhaps that of the author of the Letter to the Hebrews.

As most New Testament scholars have reservations about the historical accuracy of the first two chapters of Luke's Gospel, the two birth accounts, it is necessary to deal early with this issue. Most of the scholarly literature on John (and very little but scholarly assessments of John exist) deals with the quest for the historical John, seeking to separate what the author regards as historical fact from what the author regards as pious legend. Generally, the author is misguided on both counts because we have too little evidence to allow us to determine with certainty what was historical and because the concept of "pious legend" is one that often denies the divine inspiration of the Scriptures, assumes that kerygmatic or faith-based accounts are inherently biased by early Christian attitudes, and fails to see that the New Testament is not a work of information, but rather a work of transformation, shaped by the Holy Spirit. In this book, though we will make some comments on historical issues, we will regard the scriptural text as one that has been accepted in its final form and deal with it in terms that are more literary and theological, rather than purely historical.

At this point, it would be advisable to read the first two chapters of Luke's Gospel, a work of some 132 verses. A close reading of these two chapters will quickly reveal an astonishing fact about the literary method of Luke, the evangelist. Luke tells us in the prologue to his Gospel that he will write "an orderly account" based on oral traditions handed on by "eyewitnesses and servants of the word" (1:2–3). While we have no certainty as to Luke's sources for the birth accounts, scholarly speculation regards Mary, the Apostles and disciples of Christ, and the disciples of John the Baptist as the most likely sources. Luke devotes more attention to John the Baptist in this infancy narrative than he does in all the rest of his Gospel. We are forced to ask ourselves: Why does Luke devote his greatest attention to John in the same section where he gives his account of Jesus' nativity?

The inescapable surprise when we read these first two chapters of Luke's Gospel is the extensive care that Luke has taken in shaping parallels and doublets in his accounts. Table 1:1 is a chart of the parallel elements in the births of John the Baptist and Jesus. It shows that the entire narrative of these two births has been structured around a symmetry of the two accounts.

---

[ Table 1:1 ]

**A CHART OF THE PARALLEL ELEMENTS IN THE BIRTHS OF JOHN THE BAPTIST AND OF JESUS**

| Birth of John the Baptist | Birth of Jesus |
| --- | --- |
| Luke the historian opens with a statement dating the event: "In the days of King Herod of Judea" (1:5). | He begins in chapter two by dating Jesus' birth: "In those days a decree went out from Emperor Augustus that all the world should be registered" (2:1–2). |
| He then takes up the background of Zechariah and the descent of Elizabeth from Aaron (1:5). | He then gives the background of Joseph and his descent from the house and family of David (2:4). |

Luke notes that Elizabeth was elderly and barren (1:7). The angel Gabriel appears to a terrified Zechariah who asks Gabriel, "How will I know that this is so?" (1:18).

The angel Gabriel predicts the birth of a son to be named John (1:13).

Gabriel predicts that before his birth, John will be filled with the Holy Spirit (1:15).

The mission of John is described (1:16–17).

Elizabeth acknowledges what the Lord has done for her (1:25).

Zechariah proclaims the hymn, the Benedictus (1:67–79).

Luke records the actual birth of John (1:57–58).

Luke recounts the circumcision and naming ritual of John (1:59–64).

Luke records a number of prophecies about John (1:14–17, 76–79).

Luke summaries in one sentence John's progress from youth to maturity at the end of his infancy account of John (1:80).

At the Annunciation, a fearful Mary asks the angel Gabriel, "How can this be, since I am a virgin?" (1:34).

The angel Gabriel predicts the birth of a son to be named Jesus (1:31).

Gabriel says to Mary: "The Holy Spirit will come upon you…and the child to be born will be holy" (1:35).

The mission of Jesus is described (1:32–33).

Mary acknowledges her role as the servant of the Lord (1:38).

Mary proclaims the hymn, the Magnificat (1:46–55).

Luke records the actual birth of Jesus (2:6–7).

Luke recounts the circumcision and naming ritual of Jesus (2:21).

Luke records a number of prophecies about Jesus (1:32–33, 35; 2:11, 30–32).

Luke summarizes in one sentence Jesus' progress from youth to maturity at the end of his infancy account of Jesus (2:52). He also has an earlier summary for Jesus that more closely parallels John's in wording (in 2:40).

Luke, good historian that he is, opens his accounts by dating each event. But he dates the birth of John through King Herod of Judea—the father of Herod Antipas, who will be John's executioner. He dates the birth of Jesus through the Emperor Augustus, and it will be Roman authority, in the figure of the procurator Pontius Pilate, that will execute Jesus. Luke next gives the family background of each figure. Family or tribal identity, as expressed in that favorite biblical genre, the genealogy, was the key means of establishing a person's identity. The Hebrew emphasis was more on the community than on the individual. So Luke emphasizes John the Baptist's descent from a priestly family through both his father and his mother, and Jesus' descent "from the house and family of David," an early clue to Jesus' identity as the Messiah of Jewish expectation, according to some Hebrew traditions. Luke then parallels the appearance of the angel Gabriel, God's favorite messenger, to Zechariah first and then to Mary. The series of parallels continues in the prophecy of the birth of a son to each mother, and a designation of the son's name. The Holy Spirit fills John and comes upon Mary. The mission of each son is described, and each mother acknowledges the Lord. Zechariah's hymn, the Benedictus, is clearly shaped as a doublet to Mary's Magnificat. The recounting of the actual births, the circumcision, the naming ritual and the prophecies of each son's future are clearly developed also as parallels. Then, a one-sentence summary rounds off the parallel development.

This careful process of drawing parallels leads many scholars to use this as evidence of the lack of historicity in the account, or to argue that John and Jesus are here presented as co-redeemers. In order to discern the rationale for these parallels, we need first to review what can be learned from the whole narrative. This process of paralleling John and Christ runs through all the Synoptic Gospels and will become a central theme of this book and of the Synoptic presentation of John the Baptist. John, in his Gospel, wishes to downplay the rivalry of John and Jesus and to show John as both subordinate to Jesus and in a different role than in the Synoptics. We will try throughout this book to maintain the integrity of each Gospel's presentation of John.

Some scholars argue that chapter one of Luke's account may have come from a Hebrew source, and the narrative has a distinctly Old Testament character in its language and ideas. The birth of John seems based on Old Testament models, especially the birth stories of Isaac (Genesis 17:15–21), Samson (Judges 13:2–24) and Samuel (1 Samuel 1:1–23). There seems to have developed a set pattern for these special birth narratives:

1. The barrenness of the mother is overcome by God,
2. God or an angel appears to announce and prophesy the birth of a son,
3. Prophecies are given of the child's greatness and of what he will accomplish,
4. The child's name and its etymology is generally given. Notice how closely the account of John's birth has been shaped to that of patriarchs, judges and prophets.

The barrenness of Elizabeth is removed, the angel Gabriel appears to Zechariah and predicts that John will be great in the sight of the

Lord and will be filled with the Holy Spirit, among other predictions. But the naming of John is distinct and special. The names of Isaac, Samson and Samuel are given to them by their mothers, but God, in the person of Gabriel, bestows the controversial name of John upon the child—an honor reserved for few in the Old Testament (Abram to Abraham, Sarai to Sarah, Jacob to Israel) and only for John, Peter and, of course, Jesus in the New Testament. The etymology of the name John is not given in the text, but it is implied and meaningful, for the name John, *Yohanan* in Hebrew, means, "God has shown favor." It is as if these names were reserved from eternity for their recipients.

The element of prophecy is a dominant one in these two chapters because both in the Hebrew tradition and in that of classical biography, the birth and youth of heroic figures is related so that events and predictions can foretell their future glory. To look at what these prophecies foretell about John is to look into the mind of God and the mind of the evangelist. Let us then probe the significance of these prophecies.

1.   The angel Gabriel says to Zechariah, "You will have joy and gladness, and many will rejoice at his birth" (1:14).

Joy is a central theme of Luke's Gospel. John's elderly parents, who probably died before he was twelve, were overjoyed. Even within this chapter the prophecy is fulfilled, as Elizabeth's neighbors and relatives (undoubtedly including Mary) "rejoiced with her" (1:58). Raymond Brown, one of the most respected American Scripture scholars, has noted that one key to understanding the infancy narratives is to realize that the post-resurrection Christian perceptions of Christ as God and the consequent rejoicing are moved back to the conception and birth of Jesus (and of John). So the joy over John here is sparked by his role in salvation history.

2. "He will be great in the sight of the Lord" (1:15).

On no other figure in the New Testament is such a warm and general compliment conferred. Most prophecies predict great achievements, but this notes John's unique stature in God's eyes. It matches the compliment that Jesus will later confer on John as greatest among those born of women (Luke 7:28).

3. "He must never drink wine or strong drink" (1:15).

This prophecy seems to imply that John will be a Nazirite, or Holy One of God, a Hebrew group that separated itself from other men by not drinking wine or strong drink, by not cutting their hair and by having no contact with the dead (see Numbers 6:1–21). Samson and Samuel were described as Nazirites. We have no sure knowledge that John was a Nazirite, but this language helps predict John's asceticism and is confirmed in Luke 7:33 (see also Matthew 1:18), where John is described as "eating no bread and drinking no wine."

4. "Even before his birth, he will be filled with the Holy Spirit" (1:15).

The theme of the Holy Spirit is a strong one throughout Luke's writing—both his Gospel and his Acts of the Apostles. In fact, Acts is sometimes referred to as the "Gospel of the Holy Spirit." But we must be careful here to distinguish different meanings for the term *Holy Spirit* or *Spirit of God*. The concept of the Holy Spirit as a separate person and a member of the Holy Trinity was only established after the great Trinitarian councils of the fourth and fifth centuries. Later Christians tend to impose on the Gospels a meaning for the Holy Spirit that was not in the historical text of the first century. Just as the evangelists adopted a post-resurrection perspective in their writing of the Gospels, so too later readers have adopted a post-conciliar perspective in their interpretations. Some modern forms of biblical interpretation find this acceptable, but strict historical critics wish to stick to what they believe was the first-century meaning of the evangelist. The term *Holy Spirit of God* was regularly associated with the prophets. It was this Spirit that came upon Saul and made him a prophet (1 Samuel 10:10) and that spoke through David (2 Samuel 23:2) and that shared its Spirit with Elijah and Elisha (2 Kings 2:9–16). Later in Luke's Gospel, John is presented to us as prophet, and more than a prophet (7:28; 20:6). Luke 3:1–2 applies to John the classical description of the initiation of a prophet: "The word of God came to John son of Zechariah in the wilderness." With each of these prophecies Luke is preparing the way for what comes later in his Gospel.

5. He will turn many of the people of Israel to the Lord their God (1:16).

The verb *turn* is the Hebrew term *shubh*, regularly used for the repentance of the people (Deuteronomy 30:2; Hosea 3:5; 7:10), and this prediction embodies the central conception of John as an ascetic prophet, calling Israel to repentance.

6. "With the spirit and power of Elijah he will go before him, to turn the hearts of parents to their children, and the disobedient to the wisdom of the righteous, to make ready a people prepared for the Lord" (1:17).

This verse is a very important further specification of John's primary mission of repentance and reconciliation in the tradition of Elijah. We will discuss in a later chapter the issue of attributing to John the role of Elijah, but here we wish to emphasize that the angelic oracle is following the hypothetical source "Q" in applying to John Old Testament prophecies from Malachi, Sirach and Isaiah. This attribution is critical to the task of establishing that John is indeed the forerunner, the prophet and the messenger who was to come in order to prepare the way of the Lord. The fulfillment of these Old Testament prophecies is the authentication for John's mission. Table 1:2 illustrates the parallels between Luke's angelic prophecies in 1:17 and Old Testament prophecies.

---

[ Table 1:2 ]

**PARALLELS OF LUKE'S ANGELIC PROPHECIES IN 1:17 WITH OLD TESTAMENT PROPHECIES**

| Old Testament Prophecies | Luke's Parallels |
|---|---|
| 1) "See, I am sending my messenger to prepare the way before me, and the Lord whom you seek will suddenly come to his temple." (Malachi 3:1) | 1) "With the spirit and power of Elijah he will go before him...." (1:17a) |
| 2) "Lo, I will send you the prophet Elijah before the great and terrible | 2) "to turn the hearts of the parents to their children, and the dis- |

day of the Lord comes. He will turn the hearts of the parents to their children and the hearts of children to their parents...."
(Malachi 4:5–6)

obedient to the wisdom of the righteous" (1:17b, c, d)

"[Elijah], it is written, you are destined to calm the wrath of God...to turn the hearts of parents to their children...." (Sirach 48:10)

3) "A voice cries out:
    "In the wilderness prepare the way of the LORD, make straight in the desert a highway for our God."
(Isaiah 40:3)

3) "to make ready a people prepared for the Lord." (1:17e)

---

In all the Gospels, the fulfillment of prophecies from the Old Testament is often cited as a proof-text for the evangelists. Here the "messenger of the covenant" in Malachi is identified in Malachi 4:5 as Elijah, and like the prophet-priest Elijah, the prophet-priest John is charged with converting men before the Lord comes. The messenger in Malachi is from the house of Levi (Malachi 2:4) as is John, the son of Zechariah who was a Levite from the priestly order of Abijah (Luke 1:5). Elijah's mission of reconciliation is emphasized by both Malachi and Sirach. John's father, Zechariah, repeats two of these prophecies in the Benedictus (1:76–79), emphasizing that John will be a prophet, will go before the Lord to prepare his ways and will give the knowledge of salvation to his people by the forgiveness of their sins. Zechariah also reiterates the prophecy of Malachi and of Isaiah that John is to prepare the way of the Lord. With this one verse, 1:17, Luke has shown the fulfillment of four major prophecies and at the same time used these to anticipate John's role and to tie chapter one of his Gospel closely to the rest. These are made the leitmotif for his treatment of John. In 3:4 and 7:27, Luke echoes again the signature Isaian prophecy of 40:3. It is the keynote of John the forerunner.

Prophecy lies at the heart of these first two chapters; in fact, it is not an exaggeration to describe them as one long, extended prophecy. The first appearance of John on the scene, even before he is born, is the occasion for his first prophecy: "When Elizabeth heard Mary's greeting, the child leapt in her womb" (1:41). Remember that in 1:15 Gabriel told Zechariah that John will be filled with the Holy Spirit even in his mother's womb, and that he will be a prophet. Here John is performing from the womb his quintessential function as the forerunner—he is welcoming Jesus as the Messiah in his mother's womb and thus joyfully declaring the advent of the new age, the messianic age.

But John is not only a prophet himself; he causes his mother and father to be prophets. "And Elizabeth was filled with the Holy Spirit and exclaimed with a loud cry, 'Blessed are you among women and blessed is the fruit of your womb. And why has this happened to me, that the mother of my Lord comes to me?'" (1:41–43). Notice that Elizabeth's humility anticipates her son's humility expressed in John's Gospel as "He must increase, but I must decrease" (3:30). As the Holy Spirit is the vehicle for these prophecies, he uses the language of beatitudes ("Blessed is . . ."), which is also standard Old Testament language. But we are also here witnessing the transition that is so essential a part of John's mission, moving from Old Testament to New Testament, because the use here of the term "Lord" (*Kyrios* in Greek), is the first time that "Lord" refers to Jesus! Elizabeth is confirming the meaning of John's leap within her womb: The Messiah, the Lord, is coming!

After the controversial naming of John, the neighbors and relatives ask: "What then will this child become?" (1:66). The answer is forthcoming in Zechariah's Benedictus. Zechariah is described as "filled with the Holy Spirit," as he delivers his "prophecy" (1:67) about John. In remarkably Christian theological language that is a continuation of Elizabeth's use of "Lord" as Jesus the Messiah, Zechariah is inspired to predict of his child that he "will be called the prophet of the Most High." He "will go before the Lord to prepare his ways" and "to give knowledge of salvation to his people by the forgiveness of their sins" (1:76–77). Many of these prophecies and even their language are repeated later in the Gospel, especially in 7:26–27. Even that distinctly Lucan theological language of salvation occurs in 3:6: "all flesh shall see the salvation of God" (even though this is a quotation of Isaiah). And in 3:10–14, Luke alone among the evangelists has John give precise instructions for salvation. And in 3:3, John proclaims "a baptism of repentance for the forgiveness of sins."

Throughout this first chapter, John is filled with the Holy Spirit, and the Holy Spirit is the confirmation of his prophecies and the guide to his actions. The sanctification of John by the Holy Spirit in his mother's womb is a mark of John's vocation. He is chosen by God not by virtue of previous merits, but by God's special election. In the words that the church used to apply to John on his feast day, John is compared to the great prophet and servant of Yahweh, Isaiah: "The LORD called me before I was born, while I was in my mother's womb he named me" (Isaiah 49:1).

The history of John the Baptist has been wrapped in controversy from the beginning, as we shall explore later. But in the twentieth century, many biblical scholars relegated John to purely a figure of the Old Testament, the epoch of the Law and the Prophets, an era about which Luke has Jesus say: "The law and the prophets were in effect until John came; since then the good news of the kingdom of God is proclaimed" (16:16). These scholars would allow John a mention only in the first part of this verse. Some do not even concede that the Lucan John was a precursor of Christ. In contrast to many historical critics, it has been the intention of this chapter to establish John as the first of Christians, the forerunner of Christ, a prophet of both the Old and the New Testament. In himself, John bridges the New Testament to the Old, and serves as a boundary marker between the ages.

The purely historical view that so many biblical historical critics adhere to prevents them from seeing that the Gospels generally, and these two chapters in particular, are not historically based but rather theologically based. This does not mean that there is not a substratum of historical experience underlying Luke's exposition, it means that he has reshaped that historical experience to express his theological ideas. We must come back here to the question we asked early in this chapter: Why has Luke lavished his greatest attention on John in the very same section where he gives his extended account of Jesus' nativity? The answer, I believe, lies in his careful construction of a symmetry between the two accounts. The elaborate set of parallels is well beyond chance and betrays his attempt to identify John as closely as possible with Jesus. This effort will continue throughout the Gospel in his depiction of John (as it does also in the accounts of the other Synoptic Gospels). The rationale for these parallels, as they can be perceived in these first two chapters, are:

- the desire to show John as a coworker with Jesus in an essential part of his mission, especially to be his precursor,
- the aim of developing a deliberate tracing of parallel patterns that highlights their similarities in birth, in parents, in the fulfillment of prophecies,
- the need to establish John as a participant with Jesus in the work of salvation, and
- the opportunity to present John as the first of Christians and as both the last prophet of the old dispensation and the first prophet of the new.

Luke's development of these parallel accounts, then, establishes that Jesus and John are engaged in the common enterprise of salvation and in which John's role, as prophet and forerunner, is to announce the coming of the Messiah, and to "make ready a people prepared for the Lord."

**QUESTIONS FOR REFLECTION**

- Review Table 1:1 that charts the parallel elements in the births of John the Baptist and Jesus. This extended series of parallels could not be a function of chance and must indicate the evangelist's desire to match these two critical birth accounts. What does the evangelist accomplish by doing this?
- How can chapters one and two of Luke's Gospel be described as one, long, extended prophecy? Which of the prophecies in this account most startles you? Why?
- What are the implications of the statement that "even before his birth, he [John the Baptist] will be filled with the Holy Spirit" (1:15)?
- What was the blood relationship between Jesus and John the Baptist? What was the difference in their ages?

# CHAPTER TWO

# John in the Desert: The Apostolate of the Wilderness

The ONLY EVIDENCE WE HAVE IN THE GOSPELS THAT John spent most of his adult life in the desert (apart from his short public ministry) is the single verse with which Luke closes the first chapter of his infancy narrative: "The child grew and became strong in spirit, and he was in the wilderness until the day he appeared publicly to Israel" (1:80).

The Greek noun, *anadeiksis*, which is here translated as "appeared publicly" carries a much greater and far more significant meaning than the translator has been able to express. The word embodies a dual meaning of "reveal" and "appoint." In classical Greek, it referred to the proclamation of an election or appointment. Here it refers to the public manifestation of an event effected by divine action or decree. It is announcing the commissioning by God the Father of John the Baptist as Jesus' forerunner after his spiritual schooling in the wilderness. What we need to examine now is the nature and importance of this desert discipline, this school for forerunners.

John's parents are both described as elderly. While we do not know exactly when John went into the desert, Christian artists have ingeniously tried to close this gap in our knowledge. In one of the oldest renditions from a Greek manuscript of the eleventh century, an angel conducts the young John the Baptist up a mountain. A work by Giovanni di Paolo from a later period shows the same lonely figure of a young John, striding courageously up the mountain, into the desert. Fra Filippo Lippi has a touching scene of Elizabeth and Zechariah in their old age bidding farewell to a John who looks no more than twelve. As we examine John's life in the desert and its import, we are in a world of hypotheses and surmises, such as are expressed in these works of Christian art. But much incidental information and sound analogies can be called upon to create a probable scenario for John's life in the desert.

This period of John's private stay in the desert may have extended for twenty years, from about A.D. 8 when he was twelve to about A.D. 28 when he was thirty-two. While such dates are speculative and approximate, they show that the majority of John's life was, like that of Jesus, a hidden life. It was a long novitiate, a time of testing and growth in the spiritual life and in spiritual combat. The summary verse above says that John "became strong in spirit." I believe that this line is best interpreted as "strong in the Spirit," and that the Holy Spirit was John's tutor in desert spirituality. The Holy Spirit is mentioned three times in Luke's first chapter as applying to John and to his father and mother, each time with the same phrase that each is "filled with the Holy Spirit" (1:15, 41, 67). In another of those parallels carefully constructed by the evangelist we learn that "Jesus, full of the Holy Spirit, returned from the Jordan and was led by the Spirit into the wilderness, where for forty days he was tempted by the devil" (4:1–2). Jesus too had a novitiate of spiritual testing in the desert. And the Holy Spirit was the guide and counselor for both.

In order to grasp the full meaning of John's long stay in the desert, we must first understand the Old Testament traditions of the desert, and especially how the prophetic traditions of the desert evolve into a Christian tradition of the desert, as shaped by John the Baptist. The Old Testament has a number of different terms to describe the varieties of desert and wilderness in the Middle East, just as the Inuits have a multitude of terms to describe the various kinds of snow and ice in their Alaskan territory. The deserts of the Sahara and the Sinai and the wilderness of Judea are each of different geological composition. But the deserts of Palestine, Transjordan and Sinai all share the common designation of "tame deserts." This means they enjoy a little rainfall every winter and they are subject to sudden storms causing flash floods. The character of the desert varies greatly. The Transjordan plateau in the south is broken by a complicated network of geological faults, and the desert here consists of broad sandy corridors between towering cliffs. Sand dunes are rare and extremely small in size and restricted in locale.

In the Old Testament there are four different Hebrew words for *desert*. But the most common is *midbár* (or *erémos* in the Greek of the Septuagint and of the Gospels), a word that refers to desolate land. In Joshua 16:61 the midbár is described as a province in the time of Jehosophat comprised of six cities in the wilderness of Judah and the lower Jordan valley, south of Jericho. The description there makes this word seem to describe a specific locale, rather than serving as a generic term. Matthew describes the area of John the Baptist's preaching as the wilderness of Judea (3:1) and as an area around the Jordan river. Most scholars surmise that John's activity centered around the eastern slopes of Judea and the Jordan valley, from Bethany to Aenon near Salim, which borders the Judean slopes and offers a splendid view to the East. If this geographical surmise is correct, John's desert ministry occurred within about forty miles of his father's home in the hill country west of Jerusalem.

Even today, the dangers and discomforts of this wilderness area are many. The heat in the Jordan valley from May to September is scorching. Food was not easy to come by, hence, John's diet of locusts and wild honey. Wild animals frequented this desert wasteland: gazelles, wolves, foxes, leopards, hyenas, ostriches and lions. Saint Paul on one occasion says: "I was rescued from the lion's mouth" (2 Timothy 4:17). While Paul's use may be metaphoric, John's experience must have been quite real. The signature line that the evangelists apply to John: "the voice of one crying out in the desert" may refer analogously to the roar of the lion in the desert. It was this interpretation of that signature line which led to Mark's Gospel being represented in art by the figure of a lion. Amos the prophet, who was from Tekoa, a town ten miles south of Jerusalem and on the border of the wilderness, recounts the story of a shepherd rescuing the remains of a lamb from the mouth of a lion. When Mark describes Jesus' sojourn in the desert, he remarks that Jesus "was with the wild beasts; and the angels waited on him" (1:13). We know from 1 Kings 17:6 that when Elijah was famished at Wadi Cherith, east of the Jordan, the Lord sent ravens that fed him bread and meat, and when he escaped to the wilderness, an angel provided a cake baked on hot stones and a jar of water. So both Jesus and Elijah received angelic aid, but John, it seems, was left to fare for himself for twenty years, unless, unknown to us, the Holy Spirit scavenged some food for him. The angel says of John: "He must never drink wine or strong drink" (Luke 1:15). And later Luke has Jesus say of John: He "has come eating no bread and drinking no wine" (7:33). It is not said that John ever took the Nazirite vow to avoid strong drink, but he may well have done so, as did Samson and Samuel before him. The Rodin sculpture that pictures an emaciated John striding and preaching seems true to what we know of John's lifestyle.

The history of the wilderness runs deep in Jewish tradition. The desert has two distinctive and seemingly opposite characteristics. First, it is a dangerous, trackless country, a home for wild beasts and bandits, and the natural habitat for Satan and his evil spirits. Second, it is a place of solitude and spiritual renewal, a place to which prophets flee in order to encounter God. Very early in biblical tradition we see this twofold characteristic at work in the case of another boy who grew up in the wilderness, Ishmael. When she becomes pregnant by Abraham, Hagar, Sarah's slave, runs away to the desert to escape her cruel and jealous treatment at the hands of Sarah. The angel of the Lord finds her by a spring of water in the wilderness and predicts the future of Ishmael and the multitude of her offspring. Hagar returns to Abraham's household and gives birth to Ishmael, but Sarah insists that both Hagar and Ishmael be cast out, and they then wander about the wilderness of Beer-sheba. When her water is exhausted, Hagar hides her son under the bushes and is reconciled to the death of both Ishmael and herself. But God appears to her and shows her a well of water. God was with the boy, as he grew up in the wilderness of Paran, which is in the Sinai desert 120 miles south of John the Baptist's wilderness of Judea. We see in this the dual qualities of the dangers of drought and yet the presence of God in guiding young Ishmael for his future mission.

The call of the desert is strong from Moses on down through the prophets. Moses was leading his flock in the wilderness when he came to Horeb, the mountain of God, and saw God in the burning bush. It is in the desert that Israel meets its God for the first time. Then Moses leads his people through forty years of testing in the wilderness where this experience of the desert was a preparation and a purification for entering the Promised Land. Moses in Deuteronomy warns his people toward the end of this period of testing that afterward,

> Do not exalt yourself, forgetting the LORD your God, who brought you out of the land of Egypt, out of the house of slavery, who led you through the great and terrible wilderness, an arid waste-land with poisonous snakes and scorpions. He made water flow for you from flint rock, and fed you in the wilderness with manna that your ancestors did not know, to humble you and to test you and in the end to do you good. (Deuteronomy 8:14–16)

In the Old Testament, Yahweh dwells especially in the desert, for it is his place of testing and reward.

This lesson was not lost on the prophets of Israel, and one of the greatest, Elijah, heard the call of the desert when he was targeted for persecution by Jezebel, the unforgiving wife of Ahab. Elijah takes off from Jezreel in the Northern Kingdom to Horeb, over two hundred miles away, or as far away from Jezebel as he can go. Only a day's journey into the wilderness, he sits down under a juniper tree and begs for death. But an angel comes and feeds him cakes baked on coals and water. On the strength of this food he walks forty days and forty nights to Horeb, the mountain of God. It is here in a scene of wind, earthquake and fire that the Lord appears to Elijah and gives him his instructions for the future of Israel. The prophets are continually revealing, as Elijah does here, the sacred nature of the desert as God's dwelling place.

It is particularly at the time of the exile in Babylon (587–538 B.C.) that the desert assumes a special significance in the teaching of the prophets. Second Isaiah knew that the Israelites could not return home without crossing the Syrian desert, and he utters a

famous oracle commanding that the way be prepared for the return
from exile of the remnant of the Jews, and so that a visible expression of the Lord's presence may again be seen in Jerusalem:

> A voice cries out:
> > In the wilderness prepare the way of the Lord,
> > > make straight in the desert a highway for our God.
>
> . . .
>
> > O Zion, herald of good tidings;
> > lift up your voice with strength
>
> . . .
>
> > say to the cities of Judah,
> > 'Here is your God!'" (Isaiah 40:3, 9b–c, f–g)

The Lord is crossing the desert with his people that he may once
again rule over Judah from Jerusalem.

In the prophets and the Psalms, the desert remains a country
inhabited by demons and "the haunt of jackals, an abode for
ostriches" (Isaiah 34:13). Yet in the Book of Revelation, the
woman clothed with the sun escapes the red dragon by fleeing into
the wilderness "where she has a place prepared by God, so that
there she can be nourished for one thousand two hundred sixty
days" (12:6). Thus, in biblical tradition, the desert is a scene of
contrasts—a habitation for Satan and his demons and a place of
solitude where saints may commune with God. But the proximity
of these two enemies makes the desert the site for fierce spiritual
combat. We see this most dramatically in Jesus' confrontation with
Satan the tempter in the desert. Satan's testing of Jesus is modeled

on the testing Israel faced in its desert wanderings from Egypt to Canaan. The temptation to pride and to self-sufficiency lay at the heart of both. Jesus shows that humility, devotion to God's will, and to "every word that comes from the mouth of God" (Matthew 4:4) are crucial in this fierce hand-to-hand combat with the devil. It does not then seem far-fetched to surmise that John the Baptist in his long sojourn in the desert must have undergone severe trials that taught him the humility we see later in his attitude that "He must increase, but I must decrease." There in the scorching sands he also learned to bring forth the fruits of repentance so that he could later preach it to others. John's echoing of the prophets in his own words, and his recognition of the prophetic signs of the Messiah when Jesus said "Go and tell John what you hear and see: the blind receive their sight, the lame walk, the lepers are cleansed, the deaf hear, the dead are raised and the poor have good news brought to them" (Matthew 11:4–5), show that John was a careful reader of the Scriptures. What else would one expect of a member of a tribe of Levi, a son of a priest and himself a priest?

The desert became for John the only home of his adult life until he took up his final residence in Herod's prison at Machaerus. His desert life was one of intense prayer and fasting. We know this from comments in the Gospels. In Luke 11:1, one of Jesus' disciples said to him, "Lord, teach us to pray, as John taught his disciples." Prayer is the fountainhead of sanctity, the source of devotion to God and to his will. Saint Teresa of Avila used to say that we cannot understand the meaning of life and its fulfillment without a deep and long dedication to prayer. In his long desert sojourn,

John must have learned the rigorous discipline of prayer so well that he became the first Christian teacher of prayer. We know also from some texts already discussed that John fasted to the point where we might call him in Carolyn Bynum's words, "the first holy anorexic." His own disciples in Matthew 9:14 come to Jesus and ask: "Why do we and the Pharisees fast often but your disciples do not fast?" In Luke 5:33, it is John's bitter enemies, the Scribes and the Pharisees, who ask this question and thus, testify to John's practice of fasting. John's life of preparation in the desert was pre-eminently a life of prayer and of fasting.

But John was not the only one praying and fasting in the desert of Judea. In 1947, the greatest archaeological discovery of the twentieth century revealed to us the existence of what seemed to be a community of Jewish monks, the Qumran community of Essenes, living near the northwest tip of the Dead Sea. We know much about the Essenes, not only from their own documents (the Dead Sea Scrolls, dating from ca. 250 B.C. to A.D. 70), but also from first-century writers, such as Philo of Alexandria and Josephus, the well-known Jewish historian. This wealth of information allows us to draw a picture of the commonalities and the differences this Essene community had with John the Baptist and gives us a basis for assessing the probability of whether John himself was ever an Essene (a claim asserted both by some scholars and by the film that the Israelis show to modern tourists visiting Qumran). What gives credence to the claim that John was an Essene is the substance of what they shared in common.

John and the Essenes occupied the same areas of the Judean

wilderness, especially the area south of Jericho, east of Jerusalem and along the northwest coast of the Dead Sea. Qumran seems to have been a community of celibate males who lived communally and with no private property. They dressed in white and never procured new garments or new shoes until the old wore out. They were devout in following their Jewish prayer rituals and washings. They studied the Scriptures and meticulously avoided work on the Sabbath. Their own documents, such as the *Community Rule* (IQS), reveal a sectarian group with strict procedures for new entrants. They had found substitutes for the Temple rites because they rejected the Sadducees and their Jerusalem rule as one of hypocrisy and corruption.

In addition to sharing the same desert, both John and the Essenes observed ascetical practices, especially fasting, showed a special interest in Isaiah 40:3 ("A voice cries out: / 'In the wilderness, prepare the way of the LORD'"). They were concerned with ritual purity and immersion, emphasized sharing of property (Luke 3:11), had a special antipathy to incest (Mark 6:17–18) and had a priestly background (Luke 1:5).

But the parallels do not establish connection or establish that John was an Essene. And even within these parallels are hidden significant differences between John and the Essenes. For example, John's baptism with water (as we will discuss more fully later) was not at all like the Essenes' which was simply a removal of ritual impurity. John's was a deliberate prelude to Christian baptism: "I baptize you with water for repentance, but one who is more powerful than I is coming after me; I am not worthy to carry his sandals. He will baptize you with the Holy Spirit and fire" (Matthew 3:11). What more startling difference could there be than the contrast of Old Testament purification rituals with New Testament baptism?

John's sharing of property is not based on the establishment of a special, sectarian community like that of the Essenes. It is a pursuit of the ethical teachings of the Old Testament (for example, Ezekiel 18:5–9), a concern for the needy, and that radical commitment to love of neighbor that leads later to a Christian community that holds all things in common for the common good (Acts 4:32 ff.). John's ethic is not communal; it is seeking to be universal.

The use by both John and the Qumran community of Isaiah 40:3 shows a significant difference in interpretation. In the *Community Rule*,[1] the voice is exhorting people to prepare in the wilderness the way of the Lord, and the path to the Lord is explained as the study of the Law. In stark contrast, each of the four Gospels of the New Testament have John quoting this verse as the signature line of his vocation as the forerunner of Christ. It is the sign of John's prophetic call and not any basis for setting up a wilderness community.

The proximity of John and Qumran is one of the factors that has encouraged the notion that John may have been an Essene. But while they shared a general location in the wilderness, we have not even a hint in the Gospels that John lived in a community. Like the prophets before him, John lived in isolation, both before and after "The word of God came to John the son of Zechariah in the wilderness" (Luke 3:2). Cases of holy people living alone in the desert are rare in rabbinic literature, but one rough contemporary of John's was the Jewish ascetic, Banus, who lived in the desert but accepted Josephus as his student and disciple. In Josephus's *Life*, he recounts his time with Banus who lived quite alone, about thirty years after John, but with a lifestyle not unlike John's ("...used no other clothing than grew upon trees, and had no other food than what grew of its own accord.")[2] So there is some contemporaneous evidence for anchorite living in the first century and in the same general area as John. But what was dramatically different between John and the Essenes is that John was an itinerant ascetic and a preacher who roamed up and down "the region around the Jordan" (Luke 3:3). The best evidence we have from the Gospels suggests that John wandered from the dry, rugged terrain of the wilderness of Judea to a completely different geographical area, the river valley of the Jordan, where John later performed his baptisms, going as far north as Aenon, near Salim in Samaria (John 3:22–24). Thus, John did not really share the same desert or the same notion of settlement into a community with the Essenes.

The greatest difference between John and the Essenes lies in the nature and rationale of John's asceticism. John's life is a succession of detachments—from his family, from the companionship of society, from his disciples, from his reputation, from his life. He learned this detachment in the school of the desert where one learns those truths and those habits that can be learned only in solitude and self-abnegation. John's early departure from his elderly parents reminds us of Jesus' words: "Whoever loves father or mother more than me is not worthy of me" (Matthew 10:37). John pioneers the life of a Christian hermit. He is the first Christian to practice in the loneliness of the wilderness poverty, chastity and obedience to the will of God. Like Saint Bruno, who founded the Carthusians, he sought to find God in the most abandoned solitary place in the desert. Like Saint Anthony of Egypt, he must have suffered the fiercest temptations of the devil. Like Charles de Foucauld of our own time, he developed a fortitude that only the burning sands can teach. John lived in the wilderness in part to fulfill the prophecy of Isaiah in that he would be the voice crying out in the wilderness, and in part to demonstrate before Christ what Christ was later to preach, namely, that Jerusalem and the Temple would be replaced. We must conclude this from the fact that John, a member of the tribe of Levites, never visits Jerusalem or enters or even refers to the Temple. While this is an argument from silence, in its context it is a silence that shouts.

Obedience to God in times of severe struggle and temptation, as John must have faced in his twenty years in the desert, and as we know he faced in his public ministry, is only possible for those who lead a spiritual and austere existence. The ascetic life, as we know from the meaning of the Greek word *askesis* is a life of rigorous spiritual exercise, a time of testing and training, like that of an athlete, but in pursuit of spiritual perfection. We have seen that John's meager rations of locusts and honey and his lack of wine and bread in his diet led later artists to depict him as an angel, and led many to remark that he observed the practices of the Nazirites, even if he never took their specific vow. John is described as wearing a camel's hair garment with a leather belt around his waist (Matthew 3:4; Mark 1:6). This garb evokes the image of that Old Testament prophet and denizen of the desert, Elijah (2 Kings 1:8). John wore it not primarily because it was the clothing of a prophet but because it was the appropriate attire for repentance. It was like the sackcloth that was the attire of repentance for the king, the people and even the animals of Nineveh. (See also Luke 10:13.) The wearing of sackcloth that contrasted with the priestly white garments of the Essenes was fitting attire for one who is later to preach repentance, but who first must learn and practice it himself in the desert. John's whole lifestyle is one of total trust in God. He is the exemplar of Christ's word that if you seek first the kingdom of God, then all else will be added unto you (Matthew 6:33).

Origen, a theologian of the third century, sums up for us his view of John in the desert in his Homily 11 on Luke:

> Previous to his manifestation to Israel, John did not pass his life under the eye of his father; instead he fled the tumult of the city and the crowded metropolis and went away into the desert, where the air is purer and the sky more limpid, and God is closer. He did so in order to spend his time in prayer in the company of the angels, for the time of baptizing and preaching had not yet arrived.[3]

This testimony of the early third century shows the admiration that existed then for John's lifestyle and helped to shape that new form of Christian life—the hermit and the monk—who were to replace the martyr as Christian hero after the end of the persecutions.

Athanasius' *Life of Anthony* (ca. 357), more a work of propaganda than of history, promoted the hermitic lifestyle that John had pioneered—a life of prayer, fasting and spiritual exercises, of abstinence from meat, strong drink and elaborate dress, an austere life in poverty, chastity and obedience. In short, John the Baptist through his solitary desert existence of twenty years put in place the essential elements of Christian monasticism.

Just as John's life was an attraction for the valiant few of later generations, it became the magnet which attracted crowds "from the whole Judean countryside and all the people of Jerusalem" (Mark 1:5). Imagine the scene: Long parades of people from all over Israel are trudging across miles of barren wilderness to hear a gaunt preacher's call for repentance and proclamation of a new age! And this from a prophet who had not left the desert for twenty years! What could possibly have led them to undertake this toilsome journey to John's desert hermitage?

The magnet of John's power, and the warrant for his message, lies in John's asceticism, refined by his long search for God in the desert. Israel has been without a prophet for 450 years, since Malachi. That silence is at last broken by the voice of John the Baptist, crying out in the wilderness: "You brood of vipers! Who warned you to flee from the wrath to come? Bear fruits worthy of repentance" (Luke 3:7–8). The desert and John the Baptist reflect a complete break between the ways of God and the ways of men. Only by going into the desert for forty years could the people of Israel become the instruments of God's plan. And only by going into the desert for twenty years could John become the forerunner of Christ. A new work demanded a new beginning, and it is only after that long preparation that "the word of God came to John... in the desert" (Luke 3:2) and the people of God followed John into the desert.

## QUESTIONS FOR REFLECTION

• Imagine yourself in the Judean wilderness with John—for twenty years. What would be the values of solitude, of silence (except for the roaring of lions), of prayer, of fasting? How were these experiences the precedents for the Christian monasticism of the future?

• How startling would John's first public appearance be after twenty years in the desert? Why would people be attracted to a hermit whose austere life had been so contrary to their own?

• In what ways was John's desert experience a summary and extension of the central experiences of the Jews in their forty years of Exodus wanderings, in their return across the desert from exile in Babylon, in the desert sojourns of the prophets, especially Elijah?

## NOTES

[1] Geza Vermes, "Community Rule," IQS 8:13-16; 9:19-20, in *The Complete Dead Sea Scrolls in English*, fourth ed. (New York: Penguin, 1977), p. 101.

[2] Josephus, "The Life of Flavius Josephus," in *The Works of Josephus*, William Whiston, trans. (Peabody, Mass.: Hendrickson, 1987), p. 1.

[3] Quoted in André Rétif, *John the Baptist: Missionary of Christ* (Westminster, Md.: Newman, 1953), p. 27.

# CHAPTER THREE

# John the Preacher:
# The Voice of the Prophet

The JEWS STILL EXPECT THE MESSIAH, AND IN THEIR
synagogues they keep a Chair of Elijah, the prophet who is to come
and to announce the Messiah. They place newly circumcised male
babies into the chair in hopes that Elijah will announce this child
as the Messiah. For Christians, this Elijah has come and he is the
preacher and the prophet, John the Baptist, whose message, like
that of other prophets, was a call to repentance and to holiness. It
is Luke who tells us that "during the high-priesthood of Annas and
Caiaphas, the word of God came to John, son of Zechariah in the
wilderness" (Luke 3:2). This is the standard Old Testament language in which God commissions a new prophet as his spokesman
and messenger. What is astonishing about this is that the voice of

prophecy has been silent in Israel since the days of Malachi, the last prophet of the Old Testament, who forecast the coming of John the Baptist, the first prophet of the New Testament: "Lo, I will send you the prophet Elijah before the great and terrible day of the LORD comes" (Malachi 4:5).

It is hard to underestimate how shocking an event this must have been for the people of Israel. It is the culmination of Old Testament expectations. It is the long-awaited end of the silence of prophecy. It is the fulfillment of this crucial prophecy of the last prophet, Malachi:

> See, I am sending my messenger to prepare the way before me, and the LORD whom you seek will suddenly come to his temple. The messenger of the covenant in whom you delight—indeed, he is coming, says the LORD of hosts. But who can endure the day of his coming, and who can stand when he appears?
>
> For he is like a refiner's fire and like fullers' soap; he will sit as a refiner and purifier of silver, and he will purify the descendants of Levi and refine them like gold and silver, until they present offerings to the LORD in righteousness. Then the offering of Judah and Jerusalem will be pleasing to the Lord as in the days of old and as in former years. Then I will draw near to you for judgment; I will be swift to bear witness against the sorcerers, against the adulterers, against those who swear falsely, against those who oppress the hired workers in their wages, the widow, and the orphan, against those who thrust aside the alien, and do not fear me, says the LORD of hosts.

For I the LORD do not change; therefore you, O children of Jacob, have not perished. Ever since the days of your ancestors you have turned aside from my statutes and have not kept them. Return to me, and I will return to you, says the Lord of hosts. But you say, "How shall we return?" (Malachi 3:1–7)

This prophecy predicts the coming of the messenger to prepare the way for the Messiah, but it also articulates the themes of John the Baptist's preaching: repentance and purification, judgment and social justice. John is the prophet who will answer the great question: "How shall we return?" What an experience this must have been for those intrepid Israelites who went into the desert to hear this prophet, garbed in leather and eating a diet of locusts and wild honey! Saint John Chrysostom reflects on this experience asking what it must have been like to witness a man coming from the vastness of the desert after so many years. This image of the prophet-preacher has attracted artists throughout the centuries, so much so that it is even a more common image than that of John's baptism of the crowds. Rembrandt's *Preaching of Saint John the Baptist* (Staatliche Museum, Berlin-Dahlem) captures the crowds of all types of people who come to the desert to hear the ascetic prophet. James Tissot's *The Voice in the Desert* (Brooklyn Museum of Art, New York) evokes a redheaded firebrand preacher, crying out in the desert, and Rodin's sculpture of Saint John the Baptist depicts an itinerant ascetic who invites us to listen to his word. Each in its way captures the entrance into the history of the precursor prophet. The most definitive and defining image of John is as a prophet preaching his fiery and apocalyptic message.

(above) Rembrandt's painting of John preaching in the desert evokes the crowds, drawn from all levels of society, come to hear his magnetic words.

(right) Auguste Rodin depicts the emaciated figure of John as a prophet, striding toward his audience and inviting them to hear his word.

At last John's long period of preparation (probably about twenty years), of fasting, prayer, contemplation and reading of Scripture, especially the prophets, has come to an end and blossomed into the start of his short (probably two-year) ministry. It is striking that John's preaching ministry begins in the desert. The desert is a transitional place. It is the place where the prophets, like Moses and Elijah, went to pray and to regroup. It is the place where Satan tests the stoutest hearts, as he tempted Jesus in the desert. It is the place that breeds rebellions from which the Egyptian false prophet led thirty thousand[1] and from which Theudas led his four hundred men[2] in their assaults upon Jerusalem. The desert is the place from which Simeon Bar Kokhba led the ill-fated last Jewish revolt against Rome in A.D. 132–135. These contradictory associations that make the desert a place of contemplation, of testing and of rebellion, each play a role in the story of John the Baptist.

But the time of contemplation is over for John, and the anchorite now becomes a preacher of testing and rebellion. It is a time of testing to see if John the prophet can fulfill the prophecy made of him by his father, Zechariah: "With the spirit and power of Elijah he will go before him, to turn the hearts of parents to their children, and the disobedient to the wisdom of the righteous, to make ready a people prepared for the Lord" (Luke 1:17). It is a time of rebellion, not in the political sense in which Herod is to interpret John's words and actions later, but in the sense of a spiritual rebellion against sin, against complacency, against that perennial Jewish and human infidelity.

It is the traditional role of the Hebrew prophet to preach to the people of Israel the call to repentance and holiness. Even that strange and recalcitrant prophet, Jonah, whom Jesus invokes in the Gospels, preaches a firm message of repentance to the people of Nineveh. But John's entrance on the stage of Christian history is different from that of any other prophet. It is an event of world-shaking import, it is the announcement of a new age in the history of the world, and John's appearance is its boundary marker. John is the gateway to the Gospels. He appears early in each of the four Gospels, and in his first manifestation in the wilderness, he is introduced by his signature line, itself a conflation of prophecies from Malachi (3:1) and Isaiah (40:3), and the line that each of the Synoptic evangelists uses to introduce John, and which John the Evangelist has John speak about himself (Mark 1:2–3; Matthew 3:3; Luke 3:4; John 1:23). Significantly in Mark's Gospel, the very first one to be written, the very first sentence has this line when we assume that there is no period but a comma after the title, Son of God, because in the Greek there are no punctuation marks. Thus, the opening of Mark's Gospel would read:

> The beginning of the good news of Jesus Christ, the Son of God.
> As it is written in the prophet Isaiah,
> "See, I am sending my messenger ahead of you,
>> who will prepare your way;
> the voice of one crying out in the wilderness:
>> 'Prepare the way of the Lord,
>> make his paths straight.'" (Mark 1:1–3)

This configuration of the first three verses of Mark's Gospel in this manner gives emphasis to two important considerations. First, it makes clear that the beginning of the good news of the gospel is the appearance of John the Baptist, who is God's messenger, Christ's forerunner, the fulfillment of two prophecies, one of Isaiah's and one of Malachi's, and the proclaimer of a new Exodus, a new way out of the wilderness and into God's freedom. Second, the verses are set out, as they should be, as Hebrew poetry because they are quotations from the oracles of prophets which record the words of God himself. The poetic form serves to give the proper emphasis and solemnity to this important passage which introduces the Gospel and summarizes John's mission.

The notion of John as forerunner of Christ is linked to the conception of him as the living boundary marker of the ages. Few prophecies of the Old Testament have received such repeated and significant attention in the New Testament as the one we have been examining, one which defines John's role as the forerunner. In the ancient world, the forerunner was the messenger who preceded the chariot of the king or of the general announcing with solemnity his imminent arrival. Similarly, John was the forerunner of the unknown Messiah, the prophet of the end time, the eschatological messenger of Malachi, "coming first to restore all things" (Mark 9:12). To understand John, we must understand this role quite clearly. The idea of an unknown Messiah is quite current in the first century. It is implicit in the question John gives to his disciples to ask Jesus: "Are you the one who is to come, or are we to wait for another?" (Matthew 11:3; Luke 7:19). It is clearly expressed in John 7:27: "When the Messiah comes, no one will know where he is from." And in early Christian tradition of the second century, we even find it on the lips of Trypho in Justin's *Dialogue with Trypho* 8, 4: "But Christ—if He has indeed been born, and exists anywhere—is unknown, and does not even know Himself, and has no power until Elias come to anoint Him, and make Him manifest to all."[3]

John's role in making the Messiah known and perhaps even in making Jesus aware of his calling is also his means of declaring that "the fullness of time" (Galatians 4:4; Ephesians 1:10) has arrived. This coming of the fullness of time is at once a declaration of the completion and fulfillment of the Old Testament and the inauguration of the New Testament. John introduces a new conception of time—a time frame that is developed throughout the New Testament as a period of three epochs. The first is the end of the law and the prophets, which Jesus declares in Luke 16:16: "The law and the prophets were in effect until John came." The second is the period of Jesus' ministry from his baptism to the Last Supper. And the third and last is the period of the church from the crucifixion, resurrection and Pentecost to the end of time. This new conception of time, this new watershed in world history is proclaimed by John: "Repent, for the kingdom of heaven has come near" (Matthew 3:2), a line that Jesus is to take as his own later in the Gospels (Matthew 4:17; Mark 1:14). Thus, John stands, like the Janus of old Roman doorways, looking back at the law and the prophets of the Old Testament and looking forward to the newly revealed Messiah of the New Testament. As the Greek Orthodox

Church proclaims of John in their office of the forerunner: "You were seen, O prophet, standing between the Old and the New Testaments, manifesting their light."[4] The Gospels, however, present John firmly as a christological figure, as one subservient to Christ, who, once Christ comes, no longer has a life of his own: "He must increase, but I must decrease." This is of the utmost importance because it expresses the unique significance of John, and it destroys the arguments of all those who would see John the Baptist as solely a son of Second Temple Judaism. He is, as he describes himself later, a friend of the Bridegroom (John 3:29), a calling to which we should all aspire and one which fixes John firmly in the Christian dispensation. If we are to understand John, we must first grasp that the greatness of his mission lies in the limitless humility of his self-renunciation. The forerunner must disappear in the shadow of the King.

Now let us ask the crucial question: What exactly is the message that John the prophet preaches? He preaches a spirituality of repentance, of fasting and of prayer—a message that he shares with the other prophets. But what then are the sources of John's distinctiveness? Matthew, who was fond of structuring his Gospel around sermons, opens the public ministry section of his Gospel by giving us a sample of John's preaching. He highlights the fact that John "appeared in the wilderness of Judea, proclaiming, 'Repent, for the kingdom of heaven has come near'" (Matthew 3:1–2). The call to repentance is John's most distinctive characteristic. It was the particular note that the angel Gabriel predicted for him to his father, Zechariah: "He will turn many of the people of Israel to the Lord their God" (Luke 1:16). In Hebrew the word for repentance derives from the verb *shúbh* meaning "to turn." Repentance, then, was not merely a matter of belief, but of action. It was a turning back to God in obedience and trust and love in order to *do* his will. The Jews expected Elijah to come to restore all things, as the prophecy in Malachi 4:5–6 envisioned. It was conceived of as a mass repentance on the part of all Israel, and it was to come just before the end time or, as Malachi said, "before the great and terrible day of the LORD comes" (4:5).

Now let us take a closer look at the three notes that make John's repentance distinctive: first, he preaches a prior requirement before baptism of a repentance based on action and not on the usual Temple sacrifices; second, his repentance is a gift for all Israel, as it is the preparation of God's people; third, John's repentance is preached with a special urgency because it proclaims both the day of judgment and the imminence of the end time. Josephus, the ancient Jewish historian and one of our only sources beyond the Gospels of contemporary information about John the Baptist, provides us with some insights that we do not get in the Gospels when he comments on John's requirements before baptism:

> But some of the Jews believed that Herod's army was destroyed by God, God punishing him very justly for John called the Baptist, whom Herod had put to death. For John was a pious man, and he was bidding the Jews who practiced virtue and exercised righteousness toward each other and piety toward God, to come together for baptism. For thus, it seemed to him, would

baptismal ablution be acceptable, if it were used not to beg off from sins committed, but for the purification of the body when the soul had previously been cleansed by righteous conduct.[5]

Baptism could not be used as a substitute for repentance or "to beg off from sins committed." John understood that repentance was the first requirement for spiritual growth. It was the indispensable starting point, and thus, a preparation for the forgiveness of sins. There was a need to grow into repentance and this could only be accomplished by the soul that was first "cleansed by righteous conduct." It is for this reason that John rejects as a "brood of vipers" the Pharisees and Sadducees who come for baptism without bearing "fruit worthy of repentance" (Matthew 3:7–8). John recognized that repentance is not the work of a day, but required long practice. It is also notable that nowhere does John mention the standard Jewish practice for demonstrating repentance by animal sacrifice in the Temple. In fact, nowhere does John even mention the Temple! While the ancient prophets made Temple sacrifice secondary to righteous conduct (see Hosea 6:6), they also prescribed Temple sacrifice. But John, son of a priest of the order of Abijah, Zechariah, seems to share with the Essenes of Qumran a scorn for the Temple and its sacrifices (though the argument for this is an argument from silence in John's case). In the *Community Rule* from Qumran (IQS 9:4–5), this Essene opposition to Temple sacrifice is expressed strongly:

> They shall atone for guilty rebellion and for the sins of unfaithfulness that they may obtain loving-kindness for the Land without

the flesh of holocaust and the fat of sacrifice. And prayer rightly offered shall be as an acceptable fragrance of righteousness, and perfection of way as a delectable free-will offering.[6]

The rejection of the Temple and its sacrifices was shared by John and by the Essenes who both saw the High Priests who administered the Temple as corrupt and hypocritical. Interestingly, John's requirement of repentance before the forgiveness of sins (see Mark 1:4, John came "proclaiming a baptism of repentance for the forgiveness of sins") remains to this day a feature of the Catholic sacrament of reconciliation.

The second note of John's repentance is that it is intended as a mass repentance for all Israel. This in fact is one of the factors that brings about John's arrest and execution. As Josephus remarks in the same passage previously quoted: "When others too joined the crowds about him, because they were aroused to the highest degree by his sermons, Herod became alarmed. Eloquence that had so great an effect on mankind might lead to some form of sedition, for it looked as if they would be guided by John in everything that they did."[7] The Gospels are at pains to emphasize "the crowds that came out to be baptized by him" (Luke 3:7), right after Luke quotes Isaiah: "all flesh shall see the salvation of God" (3:6).

In the Benedictus, Zechariah defines his son's mission in terms of all Israel:

And you, child, will be called the prophet of the Most High;
>    for you will go before the Lord to prepare his ways,
to give knowledge of salvation to his people
>    by the forgiveness of their sins. (Luke 1:76–77)

Matthew gives us a more geographically oriented version: "Then the people of Jerusalem and all Judea were going out to him, and all the region along the Jordan" (Matthew 3:5). It was John's mission to prepare a people for the Lord, and this mission has not yet ended for his message as the gateway to the Gospel is still preparing the people of God to walk the road of repentance.

The third note of John's repentance is its tie to judgment, its apocalyptic urgency. In fact, it is John's proclamation of the end time: "Repent, for the kingdom of heaven has come near" (Matthew 3:2) that gives this special urgency to John's message. It must be remembered that John himself was a rabbi and the son of a rabbi. His disciples in John 3:26 address him as *rabbi* which means "teacher" in Hebrew. In Luke 3:12 the tax collectors address him as "teacher" with the Greek word for teacher, *didaskolos*. It was expected of rabbis, as Jesus expected of Nicodemus (John 3:10), that they would be well-versed in heavenly things. John's status as a Hebrew teacher helped him win disciples, and it won respect for his vigorous message of the end of days and the coming of judgment. This is such an important and distinctive part of John's message that we must investigate it at greater length.

In the rebirth of prophecy in this new age, John appears as the eschatological prophet. It was an almost universal belief that Elijah would return to earth, shortly before the appearance of the Messiah. John was the returning Elijah, as prophesied by Malachi, to be "like a refiner's fire" (Malachi 3:2): "See the day is coming, burning like an oven, when all the arrogant and all evildoers will be stubble; the day that comes shall burn them up, says the LORD of hosts, so that it will leave them neither root nor branch" (Malachi 4:1). Like Elijah and Isaiah before him, John is a prophet who is a troubler of Israel. His voice is not the voice of the Second Temple Judaism, but the voice of the new and apocalyptic age in the history of the world. Unlike the stereotype of John's voice is one that proclaims repentance, judgment, justice and hellfire, and he proclaims his message with an eschatological emphasis and apocalyptic imagery that contrasts with what are often seen as Jesus' messages primarily of mercy and love.

It is a curious surprise that the source of John's apocalyptic vehemence is a document or oral tradition known to scholars as $Q$, from the German word for "source," *Quelle*. This source preserved many of John's fiercest sayings and was quoted by both Matthew and Luke, and only by them. It is from these passages that John acquired his reputation as a preacher of apocalyptic doom. It is through these sayings that John predicts the eschatological crisis that Jesus' coming will create.

We can get a sample of the power of John's preaching by examining his metaphors. John's vehement message of judgment and the end of days is expressed in three vivid images that occur in chapter three of Matthew and chapter three of Luke, worded so similarly that they must come from that common source, Q. The images derive from nature and from agriculture, yet they have a literary origin as well. The three images are these: vipers fleeing from a wilderness fire, the felling of trees in the forest and throwing them into the fire, the winnowing process of separating the wheat from the chaff and throwing the chaff into the fire. Note that the common element in each is destruction by fire.

Life in the wilderness of the desert was a perilous existence, as Isaiah reminds us in an oracle where he describes the Negeb as "a land of trouble and distress, / of lioness and roaring lion, / of viper and flying serpent" (30:6). It is quite probable that John witnessed a number of wilderness fires that raced across the dry brush and drove vipers and scorpions scurrying to safety. Matthew uses this image to excoriate the Pharisees and the Sadducees, saying, "you brood of vipers! Who warned you to flee from the wrath to come? Bear fruit worthy of repentance" (3:7–8). The fear of punishment, especially punishment by fire, seems to be a prime motive in John's psychology.

The second image in John's repertoire is the felling of trees which are cut down and thrown into the fire. While this scene would be unlikely in the wilderness, it did occur near the Jordan river, as is recounted in 2 Kings 6:1–4. Also in the Old Testament, the cutting down of trees is a symbol of judgment (Isaiah 10:33–34), used to predict the terrifying fate that will fall upon the Assyrians. But, once again, John's image is fixed closely on judgment and punishment: "Every tree therefore that does not bear good fruit is cut down and thrown into the fire" (Matthew 3:10).

The notion of hellfire appears more frequently late in Old Testament thought, as does the notion of resurrection. They seem to grow together from the time of the book of Daniel on (ca. 250 B.C.). We even find the notion graphically expressed in what is perhaps an apocalyptic addition in the last verse of the book of

Isaiah: "And they shall go out and look at the dead bodies of the people who have rebelled against me; for their worm shall not die, their fire shall not be quenched, and they shall be an abhorrence to all flesh" (Isaiah 66:24).

And that old garbage dump where refuse was burned in the valley of Hinnon, Gehenna, occurs frequently in late Old Testament and in New Testament contexts as a symbol of hellfire and eternal damnation.

The third image John uses is the metaphor of winnowing, a common Old Testament image from a process in which the heavier and valuable grain was separated from the much lighter and useless chaff. The winnower would toss the mixture into the air with a winnowing fork and the lighter chaff would be blown away and then burned. The Old Testament frequently refers to the wicked as chaff, as in the very first Psalm which describes the wicked as "like the chaff which the wind drives away" (Psalm 1:4). But John must nail down his image in terms of rewards and punishments, and thus, he says of Christ: "His winnowing-fork is in his hand, and he will clear his threshing-floor and will gather his wheat into the granary; but the chaff he will burn with unquenchable fire" (Matthew 3:12).

John's system of rewards and punishments seems to rely primarily on fire. John knew that the Jews were a stiff-necked people, and he hoped that if he could not save them by love, he would at least be able to save some by fear. Stern warnings of future punishment are the major theme of John's preaching, as we have received it. Lest we think that this emphasis upon punishment by fire is solely an emphasis of John's, we must look back to see that John stood squarely in a tradition of the Old Testament and of later Hebrew literature:

> The Lord GOD was calling for a shower of fire, and it devoured the great deep and was eating up the land. (Amos 7:4)

> With pestilence and bloodshed I [the Lord God] will enter into judgment with him; and I will pour down torrential rains and hailstorms, fire and sulphur. (Ezekiel 38:22)

In Malachi 3:2 and 4:1 we have the references cited before to "the refiner's fire" and the day that will burn up the arrogant and the evildoers. The same tradition can be found in the Book of Enoch and the Dead Sea Scrolls. It is common for scholars to contrast John's message of fire, judgment and justice with Jesus' message of mercy and love. For this reason, it is necessary to point out how often Jesus refers to the fire of judgment:

> If you say, "You fool,'" you will be liable to the hell of fire. (Matthew 5:22)

> Just as the weeds are collected and burned up with fire, so will it be at the end of the age. The Son of Man will send his angels, and they will collect out of his kingdom all causes of sin and all evildoers, and they will be thrown into the furnace of fire, where there will be weeping and gnashing of teeth. (Matthew 13:40–42)

> You that are accursed, depart from me into the eternal fire prepared for the devil and his angels. (Matthew 25:41)

But on the day that Lot left Sodom, it rained fire and sulphur from heaven and destroyed all of them—it will be like that on the day that the Son of Man is revealed. (Luke 17:29–30)

It is important to see from this series of quotes that there is a strong continuity between John and Jesus on this matter of judgment and fire. Both prophesied a coming apocalyptic trial.

In summary, repentance which in one sense was a deeply traditional theme of Jewish piety was radically changed first by John and then by Jesus in tying their call to repentance to an apocalyptic urgency. Both proclaimed that the fullness of time had arrived and that the kingdom of heaven was at hand (John in Mark 1:15 and Matthew 3:2; Jesus in Matthew 4:17). It is this unique combination of the call to repentance and apocalyptic urgency that attracted Judean crowds and simultaneously alarmed the Jewish religious authorities.

But John's preaching was not without its positive note of hope, for the forerunner foretold the advent of the Messiah: "One who is more powerful than I is coming after me; I am not worthy to carry his sandals" (Matthew 3:11). Though some scholars do not identify this "Coming One" with Jesus, the evidence is too strong in its favor. At the messianic entry of Jesus into Jerusalem, the same line of welcome recurs in all four Gospels: "Blessed is the one who comes in the name of the Lord!" (Mark 11:9; see also Matthew 21:9; Luke 19:38; John 12:13). It also occurs in the great confession of Martha in John's Gospel: "I believe you are the Messiah, the Son of God, the one coming into the world" (John 11:27). The Coming

One is both the agent of judgment and the one who "will baptize you with the Holy Spirit and fire" (Matthew 3:11). We will take up in the next chapter the meaning of this line and the role of the two baptisms—John's and Jesus'. But here we see that John is fulfilling his role as the forerunner, as the gateway to the Gospels—he is announcing the coming of the Messiah.

Another key role of John's preaching was, in the words of his father, Zechariah, "to make ready a people prepared for the Lord" (Luke 1:17). A major obstacle for John in preparing a renewed Jewish people for the Coming One was the Jewish reliance on historic privilege as the descendants of Abraham. Thus, the very Jewish Gospel of Matthew has John reprimand his listeners with these words: "Do not presume to say to yourselves, 'We have Abraham as our ancestor'; for I tell you, God is able from these stones to raise up children to Abraham" (Matthew 3:9). The Jews sometimes relied on a sense of inherited privilege or of a "treasury of merit" stored up for them by the patriarchs, especially Abraham. Their trust in the covenant promises leads to a complacency that inhibited the development of repentance. John thus is rejecting any notion of inherited religious merit, even if that means a shift of emphasis from the communal emphasis of the Torah. For John, repentance is a matter for each individual conscience, and this notion of personal responsibility is laying the groundwork for a Christian notion of salvation in which the remission of an individual's sins and the performance of good works are initiating a move away from the Law and its prescriptions to faith in the Coming One and to the works of social justice. While in one sense John is simply repeating the teaching of the prophets that reliance on the Jewish status as the chosen people was a delusion if they defy God's law, in another sense, God could create a new people that would be judged on their faith and their merits. We remember that God once threatened to destroy all the Israelites except Moses (Exodus 32:10) and to make a great and new nation of him, a new Israel.

Thus, it is now time to ask the question: What kind of an audience did John attract to the wilderness? And how did this solitary anchorite entice his audience to come to him? We have, first of all, documented from the Gospels that great crowds of people from Jerusalem, and all Judea, and all the region along the Jordan, came to hear John, including many Pharisees and Sadducees. We also find that John singles out in his audience for special attention the wealthy, tax collectors and soldiers (see Luke 3:10–14). We learn in another context from Jesus when he is teaching in the Temple the chief priests and the elders: "Truly I tell you, the tax-collectors and the prostitutes are going into the kingdom of God ahead of you. For John came to you in the way of righteousness and you did not believe him...and even after you saw it, you did not change your minds and believe him" (Matthew 21:31–32). This passage tells us that the chief priests and the elders of the people, as well as prostitutes, were also members of John's audience. Finally we learn from Mark the startling news that even Herod Antipas, the tetrarch (popularly known as King), who ruled Galilee and part of the Transjordan from 4 B.C. to A.D. 39, enjoyed hearing John preach. "Herod feared John, knowing that he was a righteous and holy man, and he protected him. When he heard him, he was greatly perplexed; and yet he liked to listen to him" (Mark 6:20). While Herod could have heard John preach in the desert, for this was part of Herod's territory, it is more likely that he heard him preach in his own desert fortress of Macherus where John was executed farther south in Moabite country. From John's Gospel we learn that a number of Jesus' disciples were first disciples of John, certainly Andrew (John 1:40) and probably Philip (John 1:43–45), and that they came down from Bethsaida, just northeast of the Sea of Galilee to just north of the Dead Sea, a journey of about eighty miles. What this account tells us is that John drew his audience from all areas of Palestine and from all classes of people, including those who were sinners by profession, like tax collectors and prostitutes, as well as some later to be numbered among Jesus' apostles.

Beyond the general message of repentance, what messages did John preach to his various constituencies? It is important to recognize that John is a radical reformer. He is demanding a complete turning away from sin and from the past. He is abandoning Temple and Torah for a new route to salvation, and that route, that path which John is making straight, is a new highway to Christ. His radical new message as the forerunner is to anticipate Christ in the role prophesied by Zechariah: "You will go before the Lord to prepare his ways, / to give knowledge of salvation to his people" (Luke 1:76–77). The result of this profound new message, as we heard from Josephus, was to turn everybody to John, "for they were aroused to the highest degree by his sermons."[8] John's exhortations were the first preaching of the good news to the people. But John pulled no punches. His words were full of bad news also—of judgment and justice and hellfire. His moral prescriptions for particular segments of society lay a basis for the ethics of early Christianity. But there are many scholars, especially of the historical critical school, who dispute the authenticity of Luke 3:10–14, the passage that gives ethical guidance to three segments of society, and a passage that occurs only in Luke. Rudolf Bultmann, a major twentieth century biblical scholar, regarded as absurd the notion that soldiers would have gone on a pilgrimage to John in the desert. But it may have been Jewish soldiers in the service of Herod Antipas. Is that any more absurd than a gentile Roman centurion coming to Christ to heal his slave? (see Luke 7:1–10). There is a whole group of scholars who, in their quest for the historical John, wish to see him only as a son of Second Temple Judaism and wish to regard any evidence to the contrary as Christianizing John's message. Let's look at John's messages here, and then we will turn later to this issue of the Christianizing of John's message.

In this passage, unique to Luke (3:10–14), we see John preaching his moral exhortations to the crowds, to toll collectors and to soldiers. The context is one of eschatological urgency, as John has just finished his prophecies of punishment by fire. So John is trying to advise each group of the concrete actions they should perform, appropriate to their place in life and necessary to achieve righteousness and to "bear fruits worthy of repentance." This counsel is the most extensive example we have of John's preaching on morality and daily conduct.

Note that the beginning of this passage is the crowd's question, eliciting ethical guidance: "What then should we do?" (Luke

3:10). So it is clear that the crowds look to John as a moral teacher, a rabbi or *didaskolos*. His first admonishment is to the rich or to those who have excess goods, either of property (two tunics) or of food. Share these with the poor, with those who have none. This is the earliest point in the gospel narratives that we hear that fundamental Christian imperative of caring for the poor. In this respect, John both echoes the Old Testament ("those who oppress the poor insult their Maker, / but those who are kind to the needy honor him" [Proverbs 14:31]) and anticipates the New Testament ("Blessed are you who are poor, for yours is the kingdom of God" [Luke 6:20]). Note that John's admonitions specify works of both economic and spiritual reform. For the poor in ancient countries where there were no social welfare agencies, it was the responsibility of the rich to support the poor. The very same act has a spiritual value for the rich, as it bears fruit worthy of repentance. We have here then the beginnings of a fundamental tenet of Christian spirituality. And it is essential because, as we learn from the judgment scene in Matthew 25:31–46, we are to be judged on the basis of sins of omission, of failing to clothe the naked and feed the hungry. So John is laying out here a basis of Christian ethical conduct that Jesus will also later reiterate: detachment from possessions and support for the poor.

The second group that John addresses is a notorious class of sinners in Hebrew society and one of the most despised. "Teacher, what should we do?" (Luke 3:12) ask the tax collectors. He said to them, "Collect no more than the amount prescribed for you" (Luke 3:13). Tax collectors had a reputation as money-grubbers and as extortionists and were regarded as unclean. Yet note that John does not tell them to cease being tax collectors. Many tax collectors became rich by collecting more than they were officially prescribed to collect. The system was rife with bribery and extortion. The job was secured by the highest bidder. Once the toll collector collected his prescribed toll, plus his own profit, he could try to exact whatever further income he could get. John was saying that if one wished to be righteous, he should exact no more than was prescribed. Be scrupulously fair and even a tax collector can win salvation. Here too there is a close correspondence between John's teaching and Jesus. It is, in fact, in this very Gospel of Luke that we also get two examples of tax collectors praised by Jesus. The first is in the parable of the Pharisee and the tax collector praying in the Temple, where the tax collector who would not even look up to heaven repeats his prayer, "God, be merciful to me, a sinner" and he is exalted for his humility (Luke 18:9–14). The second is that of Zacchaeus—the rich, chief tax collector who promised half his possessions to the poor, and if he had defrauded anyone, to pay back four times as much (Luke 19:1–10). Once again John's ethical concerns for the tax collectors are echoed by Jesus.

The third class that John addresses is the surprising class of soldiers whom he advises: "Do not extort money from anyone by threats or false accusations, and be satisfied with your wages" (Luke 3:14). The stereotype of the soldier, Roman or Jewish, was of being a cruel and expert extortionist (a reputation continued in Hollywood movies), and at the same time a malcontent never satisfied with his wages. John's advice is parallel to his earlier exhortations: Avoid the common temptations of your vocation and cultivate both contentment and a detachment from riches. This theme of detachment from riches we hear from Christ in word and in example but nowhere more poignantly than in the case of the rich young man who would not follow Christ because "he was very rich" (Luke 18:23).

There is the fourth class of sinners that we know was in John's audience from a different context: prostitutes. Jesus tells the chief priests and elders: "Truly I tell you, the tax-collectors and the prostitutes are going into the kingdom of God ahead of you. For John came to you in the way of righteousness and you did not believe him" (Matthew 21:31–32). Did John in this case ask them to abandon their profession? We do not know. But it would be shocking if he did not. Jesus in the case of the adulterous woman in John 8:1–11 tells her to go and sin no more, though he does not direct the Samaritan woman who is living with one who is not her husband to leave him (John 4:16–19), but the focus of that passage lies elsewhere. What we learn from this passage is that women were part of John's followers, and they accepted his moral advice and would, therefore, precede the chief priests and the rulers into the kingdom of God.

As we conclude our examination of this sample of John's preaching, we must observe that John is preaching primarily to the despised sinners of Hebrew society: the indifferent wealthy, the greedy tax collectors, the extortionist soldiers and the ubiquitous prostitutes. He has come, like Jesus, to preach not to the self-righteous but to sinners and to make of them a new people of God.

As we stated before, it is our intention in this book to high-light, as do the Gospels, the parallels in teachings and in events between John and Jesus. Here we wish to demonstrate many of the close parallels in teaching and even in wording between the two.

The emphasis on repentance and the use of the key line "Repent, for the kingdom of heaven has come near" occurs early in the ministry of each (John in Matthew 3:2; Jesus in Matthew 4:17; see also Mark 1:15). As we review these parallels, note how often the words of John are echoed exactly by Jesus. Sometimes, however, it is an echo of the idea rather than of the words, as occurs with John's metaphor, "the axe is lying at the root of the trees" (Matthew 3:10; Luke 3:9)—a phrase which John uses to symbolize judgment in the burning of trees. Jesus uses not the same phrase but the same idea when he says, "Every tree that does not bear good fruit is cut down and thrown into the fire" (Matthew 7:19). A similar use of the echo of ideas is the repetition by Jesus of John's warning that the Jews should not rely on their descent from Abraham as the route to salvation (John in Matthew 3:9 and Luke 3:8). Jesus admonishes the Jews, "If you were Abraham's children, you would be doing what Abraham did" (John 8:39). The expressive image, "You brood of vipers!" (John in Matthew 3:7 and Luke 3:7) occurs on Jesus' lips twice later in Matthew (12:34; 23:33), and in all three cases the image is used to describe the Pharisees. The sharing of tunics, which John prescribes (Luke 3:11), is echoed in concert by Jesus in Matthew 5:40 and Luke 6:29.

The themes that John and Jesus share in common are many. The theme of hellfire that we encountered in John's metaphors is

a staple of Jesus' warnings ("You will be liable to the hell of fire";
[Matthew 5:22; see also 5:29, 30; 16:28; 18:9; Mark 9:43–47]), and
all of this in both cases warns of the coming apocalyptic trial.
Similar to this is John's theme of the wheat and the chaff
(Matthew 3:12; Luke 3:17), which receives its echo in Jesus' para-
ble of the wheat and the tares (Matthew 13:24–30, 36–43), of the
dragnet (Matthew 13:47–50) and of the sheep and the goats
(Matthew 25:31–46). The close relationship of righteousness and
judgment, so prominent in John's preaching, is also expounded in
Matthew's Sermon on the Mount (5:1—7:27) and in Luke's
Sermon on the Plain (6:17–38). There also we find echoes of
John's detachment from possessions and his care for the poor.
John's teachings anticipate much that will appear again in the
ethics and theology of early Christianity.

Like Jesus, John early endures the opposition of the chief
priests, the Levites, the elders and the Pharisees in general. The
question asked by the priests and the Levites sent by the Pharisees
in John 1:25, "Why then are you baptizing if you are neither the
Messiah, nor Elijah, nor the prophet?" is echoed by the same
priests and the Levites in Mark 11:28 when they challenge Jesus,
"By what authority are you doing these things?" Thus, the confrontation between Jesus and the Pharisees that mounts to a cli-
max in the Gospels begins with their challenge of John's authority
and mission.

The last element we must consider in reference to John's
preaching is the contention by historical scholars that the portrayal we have of John in the Gospels is grossly distorted because

the early church and the evangelists were at pains to "Christianize" the message and figure of John the Baptist. For over two centuries now some scholars have mounted a campaign to separate the Jesus of history from the Christ of faith. Now they are engaged in an effort to separate the John of history from the Baptist and forerunner of faith. I will cite here as typical the arguments of one historical scholar, Joan Taylor in *The Immerser: John the Baptist within Second Temple Judaism*. Such scholars see John as primarily a figure of Second Temple Judaism. They contend that the Gospel accounts, especially but not exclusively John's Gospel, attempt to reverse the subordination of Jesus to John. They regard Luke's infancy narratives as legend and then want to conclude that "John has no background; he simply appears (cf. Matt 3:1)."[9] While rejecting much of the text about John as myth and arguing that "[t]he Gospels' depiction of John was designed to sever him from the Jewish world around him," they then create a social context for John out of what they admit as "at best good guesswork." Thus, we have a hermeneutics of suspicion pitted against a hermeneutics of the text.

If John is not a figure who is tied to Christ and to the church, then he is a figure of no importance, a minor figure from the *Antiquities* of Josephus. To see John as only or primarily a figure of Second Temple Judaism is to miss his significance entirely both in the Gospels and in Christian history. It is even to distort his Old Testament roots, to deny the prophecies of Malachi and to negate the prophecies of his father Zechariah, inspired by the Holy Spirit (Luke 1:67). This course minimizes John's role as prophet and precursor, and without positive evidence, contradicts the role given John in the four Gospels and in Acts. Such exegesis can make no sense of John's stay in the desert. Joan Taylor offers: "In terms of history, however, John's context cannot have been simply the desert. He cannot have come into existence in some magical way as a voice in the wilderness calling people to look towards Jesus. This is the stuff of myth. The real John was probably far more a man of his age. We can assume...".[10] In such fashion do some historical scholars substitute their own assumptions and hypotheses for the clear meaning of the text.

We should also consider the fact that some eyewitnesses who heard John in A.D. 29–30 would still be alive to refute evangelists' statements in A.D. 80–90. But the ultimate argument that defeats the case for the Christianizing of John is the event for which he is most famous—the baptism of Jesus. This event, as we will see in the next chapter, is both puzzling and embarrassing for Christians. Why would a sinless Jesus need to be baptized at all? Those scholars who wish to see John as merely a Jewish teacher of righteousness and the Gospels as mere Christian propaganda miss the real Christian adaptation that lies in applying to John the Old Testament prophecies which give him the role of Elijah (Malachi 3:1, 23; Isaiah 40:3) and which then sees John's preparatory role as the precursor of Christ. He has become, as the noted Catholic scriptural scholar Raymond Brown calls John, "an incipient Christian." To miss this is to miss his significance.

## QUESTIONS FOR REFLECTION

- The coming of John the Baptist establishes a new conception of time. Explore this conception. Why was it needed? How is John himself the boundary marker for this new era? How does this concept relate to the biblical phrase, "the fullness of time"?

- John, the preacher of repentance, teaches us that repentance is not the work of a day, but requires long practice. How can we apply this in our lives? And how is repentance the precursor's royal and necessary road to Christ?

- Imagine John the Baptist as a television evangelist, proposing works of both economic and spiritual reform and not hesitating to denounce public figures who were involved in public scandal. How do you think his preaching would be received, if he returned today to proclaim his messages of repentance and fiery judgment, of hope in the Messiah and of social justice?

## NOTES

[1] See Flavius Josephus, *The Jewish War*, G.A. Williamson, trans. (New York: Penguin, 1981), pp. 261–263.

[2] Josephus, *Antiquities of the Jews*, XX (Cambridge, Mass.: Harvard University Press, 1965), pp. 97–99. See also Acts 5:36.

[3] Justin Martyr, "Dialogue with Trypho," in *The Ante-Nicene Fathers*, volume one (Grand Rapids, Mich.: Eerdmans, 1989), p. 199.

[4] Sergius Bulgakov, *The Friend of the Bridegroom: On the Orthodox Veneration of the Forerunner*, Boris Jakim, trans. (Grand Rapids, Mich.: Eerdmans, 2003), p. 4.

[5] Josephus, *Antiquities of the Jews*, XVIII–XX, pp. 81–82.

[6] Vermes, "Community Rule," IQS 9:4–5, p. 101.

[7] Josephus, *Antiquities of the Jews*, XVIII, 5, 2, p. 83.

[8] Josephus, *Antiquities of the Jews* XVIII, 5, 2, p. 83.

[9] Joan Taylor, *The Immerser: John the Baptist within Second Temple Judaism* (Grand Rapids, Mich.: Eerdmans, 1997), p. 12.

[10] Taylor, p. 12.

# CHAPTER FOUR

# *John the Baptizer: Witness to the Trinity*

One OF THE ETERNAL FASCINATIONS OF JOHN THE
Baptist is that he is an enigma in the New Testament. His mystery
lies partly in his status as "Baptizer" and as forerunner. The title by
which he is known to history, John the Baptist, is itself an anomaly.
The Greek word *baptistes* seems to be one coined especially for
John. It occurs only in Josephus and in the Synoptic Gospels.
While it was a Jewish custom to distinguish between people of the
same name by adding another name (for example, Simon Peter,
Simon the Zealot, Simon of Cyrene, Simon Magus), here the point
of the surname seems to be an attempt to define John by his most
distinctive and defining activity. The Greek word *baptizo*, from
which "Baptist" is derived, means "to dip or immerse in water" with

a connotation of cleansing. The fact that the word or title *baptist* is not used elsewhere—not in any secular context, nor even in the Gospel of John or in Acts suggests that it is a Jewish-Greek formation designed solely to describe this strange and unique activity of John. The title is often used in its participial form, the one baptizing *(o baptizón)*, to emphasize that what John does is a strange activity indeed. This is rarely understood, but it is essential to comprehend that what John was doing, baptizing, was totally different from the multitude of Jewish bathing rituals and lustrations. It is the mistake of many to confuse John's baptism with the various immersions prescribed in the Torah. When Josephus joined his mentor, Banus, a desert ascetic like John, he watched Banus bathe often in cold water by day and by night.[1] From the Dead Sea Scrolls we learn that the Essenes at Qumran had bathing facilities for ritual purification and many rules for such bathing.

The distinctiveness of this title, Baptist, is confirmed by the fact that it was conferred on him in John's own lifetime through its use by Jesus (Matthew 11:11), by his own disciples (Luke 7:20), by Herod (Matthew 14:2), by the daughter of Herodias (Matthew 14:8) and by Herodias (Mark 6:24). John himself remarks that his divine commission comes from "the one who sent me to baptize with water" (John 1:33). The Pharisees and scribes never use this title because they questioned John's right to baptize, as they associated baptism only with the Messiah (Ezekiel 36:25; Zechariah 13:1).

But what must be examined is the issue of what made John's form of baptism unique. It is, first of all, the fact that John himself administers the rite. Ritual purity was very important for Second Temple Judaism, and in the Dead Sea Scrolls we find the descriptions of many different rites of ritual purification by bathing. These might take place in the Jordan River, in any body of water or in a *miqveh*, a bathing pool cut into the rock, many of which have been uncovered not only at Qumran but throughout the land of Israel. But in all these rituals, even what is sometimes referred to as Jewish proselyte baptism, or the immersion of converts to the Jewish faith, the individual bathes himself and has no administrator or baptist. Also, the rite is viewed solely as a means of bodily purification.

Another element that makes John's baptism distinctive is the fact that it is a new rite, one that did not derive from the Old Testament prescriptions of ablution. This rite was not private, but a very public rite, making John a new lawgiver. He leaves behind the ritual laws and the sacrifices for repentance, done in the Temple by a hereditary Levite. The result of John's baptism is a new and resurrected person who has left behind his old life and has embarked on a new journey and has made a public proclamation of this new birth, achieved through God but with the agency of this new and eschatological figure, the Baptist.

What also makes John's baptism different is that his is a rite that symbolized inner moral cleansing achieved through prior repentance and that constituted initiation into a new community. John seems to make it a preparation for the end time, or as one scholar calls it, "an eschatological sacrament, the last preparation and sealing of the baptized for the coming 'baptism' of the

Messiah." John's baptism appears to have been administered only once, whereas Jewish immersions were constantly repeated. So John's baptism seems to have marked a person in some special way that was indicative of a conversion and an initiation and was not repeatable. A rare description of a baptism in the New Testament, one which seems to have more resemblance to John's than to later Christian baptism, is that recounted in Acts 8:38–39, where Philip baptizes the Ethiopian eunuch. Both enter the water, Philip administers the baptism, and the eunuch goes on his way rejoicing. The passage has all the marks of a Johannine baptism: an act of conversion, an administrator, an initiation and after the presumably one-time event, the Ethiopian heads off for home rejoicing. But this baptism is one of the first instances of Christian baptism and shows us the transition from one to the other, as the Ethiopian goes off rejoicing, a sign of his receiving the seal of the Holy Spirit which produces rejoicing and spiritual joy. Christian baptism looks back to the baptism of John and is a continuation and fulfillment of John's mission. The remission of sins cannot be bestowed until Christ's blood of the covenant has been shed for many (Matthew 26: 28). Thus, Philip is here performing the first Christian baptism recorded in the New Testament.

It has been argued by some that Josephus's account of John's baptism shows it to be only a typical Jewish ablution. But such a view fails to account for the fact that Josephus gives John his unique title of "Baptist" as the administrator of the ritual, a role never applied to other Jewish ablutions, and Josephus tells us that John required a previous cleansing of the soul by righteous conduct.[2] Josephus's account of John's baptism, written about A.D. 90, shows in fact a remarkable grasp of some of the distinctive elements in John's baptism.

We need to examine that central act of John's public ministry, his baptism of Jesus in the Jordan River. This event is so central to John's role as Baptist and as forerunner that we will examine it at length by scrutinizing the accounts of one of the very few events that occur in all four Gospels. An illuminating way to do this which will highlight the significant differences in each account is to lay the passages side by side as scholars do when they use a book of Gospel parallels, or a synopsis, as it is called.[3]

---

## [Table 4:1]

### THE BAPTISM OF JESUS: THE GOSPEL ACCOUNTS

#### Matthew 3:13–17

Then Jesus came from Galilee to John at the Jordan, to be baptized by him. (3:13)

John would have prevented him, saying, "I need to be baptized by you, and do you come to me?" (3:14)

But Jesus answered him, "Let it be so now; for it is proper for us in this way to fulfill all righteousness." Then he consented. (3:15)

And when Jesus had been baptized, just as he came up from the water, suddenly the heavens were opened to him and he saw the Spirit of God descending like a dove and alighting on him. (3:16)

And a voice from heaven said, "This is my Son, the Beloved, with whom I am well pleased." (3:17)

## Mark 1:9–11

In those days Jesus came from Nazareth of Galilee and was baptized by John in the Jordan. (1:9)
And just as he was coming up out of the water, he saw the heavens torn apart and the Spirit descending like a dove on him. (1:10)
And a voice came from heaven, "You are my Son, the Beloved; with you I am well pleased." (1:11)

## Luke 3:21–22

Now when all the people were baptized, and when Jesus also had been baptized and was praying, the heaven was opened and the Holy Spirit descended upon him in bodily form like a dove. (3:21–3:22a)
And a voice came from heaven, "You are my Son, the Beloved; with you I am well pleased." (3:22)

## John 1:29–34

The next day he saw Jesus coming toward him and declared, "Here is the Lamb of God who takes away the sin of the world! (1:29)
This is he of whom I said, 'After me comes a man who ranks ahead of me, because he was before me.' (1:30)
I myself did not know him; but I came baptizing with water for this reason, that he might be revealed to Israel." (1:31)

And John testified, "I saw the Spirit descending from heaven like a dove, and it remained on him. (1:32)
I myself did not know him, but the one who sent me to baptize with water said to me, 'He on whom you see the Spirit descend and remain, is the one who baptizes with the Holy Spirit.' (1:33) And I myself have seen and have testified that this is the Son of God." (1:34)

---

Let us examine first the account in Mark, the earliest of the four Gospels, written probably in the late A.D. 60s. In Mark's compressed Gospel it is wise to read it from the end backward. And here in this introductory narrative of Jesus' baptism, we must look back to see the context for this story. As we saw before, the beginning of the good news is the advent of the messenger who proclaims the Messiah's coming, one called the Baptist: "I have baptized you with water but he will baptize you with the Holy Spirit" (1:8). In Mark, the Baptist traditions are subservient to the Jesus traditions for, "He must increase, I must decrease," as John says later. Once John is confirmed as the forerunner in the prophecies of 1:1–8, then Mark can proceed because he has in these few early verses established John as the prophet of the end time, the eschatological messenger of Malachi and the boundary marker for a new age.

Then Mark recounts the event with directness and utter sim-plicity: "Jesus...was baptized by John in the Jordan." This is the earliest account we have of Jesus' baptism, and it shows absolutely no embarrassment that the sinless Jesus is submitting to a baptism of repentance for the forgiveness of sins! Note too that in this

Marcan account it is Jesus and Jesus only who experiences this vision and hears the voice of the Father in the first account in Christian history of the gathering of the Trinity. Jesus himself then must be the primary source for this description of the heavens opening, the Spirit's descent as a dove and the heavenly voice.

Now, let us turn to what is perhaps the second account of Jesus' baptism, written probably in the late A.D. 70s or early 80s. Here we encounter a radically different version, and a version that is noticeably longer than the others, because for Matthew the awkwardness and embarrassment of Jesus' being baptized is a major problem. As a result, Matthew records John's objection to this event which was to become a signature event of John's ministry: "John would have prevented him [from being baptized], saying, 'I need to be baptized by you, and do you come to me?' But Jesus answered him, 'Let it be so for now; for it is proper for us this way to fulfill all righteousness.'" This is one of those puzzling exchanges, or hard sayings, as they are sometimes dubbed, which require careful exegesis.

This baptism of Jesus has posed problems both for early Christians and for later Christian theology. The problem of the early church with this passage is best expressed in passages from two of the later apocryphal gospels. In the *Gospel According to the Hebrews* we find this passage:

> Behold the mother of the Lord, and his brethren said unto him, John the Baptist baptizeth unto the remission of sins; let us go and be baptized of him. But he said unto them: Wherein have

I sinned that I should be baptized of him, unless peradventure this very thing that I have said is a sin of ignorance?[4]

This passage reflects the great question of both the ancient church and modern theology: Why did Jesus need to be baptized?

In the second apocryphal gospel, the *Gospel of the Ebionites*, the writer has John, after he has baptized Jesus, see a great light, fall down before him and say: "I beg you, Lord, baptize me." This second passage raises the question of what is the difference between John's baptism and the later baptism of Christ, or Christian baptism? This enigma seems buried also within Jesus' response to John in Matthew: "Let it be so for now; for it is proper for us in this way to fulfill all righteousness" (3:15).

Matthew alone records embarrassment at Jesus' baptism and Matthew alone expresses Jesus' own rationale for the baptism. Mark's theologically naïve account probably caused confusion in the early church, a confusion Matthew was attempting to clear up. So how does he do that? First, he sharpens the distinction between Jesus and John, so that only Jesus is seen as the Messiah. Second, he deletes Mark's reference to the forgiveness of sins. Matthew 3:11 recounts these words of John: "I baptize you with water for repentance, but one who is more powerful than I is coming after me; I am not worthy to carry his sandals. He will baptize you with the Holy Spirit and fire." In Matthew's Gospel only the blood of Christ brings about forgiveness (26:28—This is my blood of the covenant, which is poured out for many for the forgiveness of sins.") Third, Matthew's baptism is no longer a private vision, nor is it simply about individual sin. It is a means of relating Jesus' own righteousness to the whole people publicly. It is a confirmation of John's program for the restoration of Israel.

John recognizes Jesus' superiority when he objects: "I need to be baptized by you" (3:14). But Jesus will not let that humility stand without qualification: "It is proper for us in this way to *fulfill* all righteousness" (3:15, emphasis added). This rationale of Jesus' is the key to understanding this passage. John is a partner with Jesus in fulfilling the will of the Father, albeit a junior partner. The Greek word for righteousness, *dikaiosune,* is one of Matthew's favorite words for designating the faith of Christians (see his use of it in the Beatitudes [5:6, 10]). It is a sound principle to explain Scripture by Scripture, and the best explanation of this verse may lie in Paul's assertion: "So we are ambassadors for Christ, since God is making his appeal through us; we entreat you on behalf of Christ, be reconciled to God. For our sake he made him to be sin who knew no sin, so that in him we might become the righteousness of God" (2 Corinthians 5:20–21). This remark of Paul's helps us to see that Jesus by being baptized by John is giving a new and more elevated meaning to John's rite. By Jesus' act, John's baptism is fulfilled (*plerosai,* to fulfill, is another favorite word of Matthew's); it is marked with the authority of Christ; its fulfillment is at the same time its transformation. Rudolf Bultmann, one of the great biblical scholars of the twentieth century, commented that, "Jesus was the first who received the Baptism of water and the Spirit, and by that inaugurated it as an efficacious rite for believers."[5] For this reason, we see the first pub-

lic witness to the Trinity—because it confirms the divine author-
ization of the baptismal rite, as established here by the Messiah.
Thus, John's baptism in Matthew becomes not just a preparation
of the way, but an indispensable part of the way. By his baptism,
Jesus makes John and the people of God whom John baptizes a
part of the Christian dispensation, because their forgiveness now
derives from the Messiah, the Suffering Servant in whose future
death on the cross all baptism will find its fulfillment.

Now, let us turn to Luke's account of John's baptism of Christ.
Luke in his Gospel places more emphasis on the baptizing ministry
of John than he does on John's baptism of Christ. In Acts 1:22,
when the apostles wish to replace Judas as one of their number,
they make it the essential criterion that such a replacement must
be "one of the men who have accompanied us throughout the time
that the Lord Jesus went in and out among us, beginning from the
baptism of John until the day when he was taken up from us."
Thus, John is clearly set up as the initiator of the period of fulfillment, the central epoch in the history of salvation. But in Luke's
account of Jesus' baptism, the briefest of the four accounts, he
seems not to know what to make of John's role. As a result, he
buries it in a subordinate clause that recounts both the baptism and
the fact that Jesus was praying: "when Jesus also had been baptized
and was praying" (3:21). It is not even stated that John baptized
Jesus, as was true in Mark's and Matthew's accounts. Luke seems
much more intent on recounting the event of the opening of the
heavens, the descent of the Holy Spirit as a dove and the voice
from heaven, though it is not clear whether this is a public event,

or one witnessed only by Jesus. It may be that Luke does not know what to make of the baptism of Jesus by John. Alternately, he might have designed his account to emphasize the witness to the Trinity. Of course, it may well be that we simply do not grasp what purpose Luke had in mind.

In the Gospel of John, as so often in this unique Gospel, we get the strangest account of all. Here, John never baptizes Jesus, nor is John ever called the Baptist. There is a rivalry in John's Gospel between the disciples of John and the disciples of Jesus (some of whom—Andrew, and probably Philip—were former disciples of John). This rivalry shows in the evangelist's efforts to keep John subordinate to Jesus. The evangelist does this in part by changing John's role from that of Baptist to that of witness, a subject we will take up in a later chapter. But here the same factors that caused Matthew and Luke to revise Mark's account have caused this evangelist to omit the scene of Jesus' baptism by John altogether and to concentrate his account elsewhere. When the evangelist witnesses to the fact that Jesus is "the Lamb of God who takes away the sin of the world" (1:29), he makes clear that John's baptism is no longer needed for the forgiveness of sins, and he creates a contrast between John who came baptizing with water (1:26) and Jesus "who baptizes with the Holy Spirit" (1:33). It is as if the evangelist wants us to see that John's baptism was solely for the purpose of convincing the world of its need for purification, but a purification that only Christ could bring. Therefore, when the evangelist insists that the Holy Spirit remained with Jesus (1:32), he is drawing a contrast between the water purifiers (both John and the Jews—cf.

2:6) and Jesus who has the Holy Spirit and will give it to his own (see 3:5). Here too, the evangelist makes the appearance of the Trinity a very public event about which he says: "John testified" (1:32), for both John's role as a witness and the development of the concept of the Trinity are central to John's Gospel.

The omission of any direct account of Jesus' baptism shows how acutely embarrassed the Christian community was by this event. It seems almost imperative for John's Gospel with its high Christology (an emphasis on Jesus as God) to omit or downplay the event. There were Baptist sectarians who argued for the Baptist's superiority over Jesus, and this factor conditioned the evangelist's narrative. So the evangelist keeps not the baptism, but this first appearance of the Trinity, for the Jordan River is the first site of our Trinitarian knowledge of God.

The wider meaning of this whole event is what makes John's baptism of Jesus the chief event of John's public ministry. To probe this wider meaning, we must first see that what is really transpiring here is the Messianic anointing of Jesus with the Holy Spirit. The term *Christ*, which later became used as Jesus' last name, was first his title—*Christos* in Greek, "the anointed one," and in Hebrew, *mashiah*, "the Messiah." But if this august title, "the anointed one of God," was conferred upon Jesus, the question arises: when and how was he anointed? A little background will be helpful. In the Old Testament it is primarily kings who are anointed, as Saul, the first king of Israel, was by Samuel (see 1 Samuel 10:17), and as David was anointed also by Samuel (1 Samuel 16:12–13). Some priests were also anointed, as Aaron was anointed by Moses (Leviticus 8:12). Anointing was a means of investing someone with power and often signified their consecration for some holy purpose. In the New Testament, apart from the use of the title, Christ, there are two references, both in Acts, to the public anointing of Christ. The first occurs after Peter and John were released by the Sanhedrin. They pray with a prayer taken from Psalm 2:1–2, which records a situation parallel to theirs:

> Sovereign Lord, who made the heaven and the earth, the sea, and everything in them, it is you who said by the Holy Spirit through our ancestor David, your servant:
>> "Why did the gentiles rage,
>>> and the peoples imagine vain things?
>> The kings of the earth took their stand,
>>> and the rulers have gathered together
>>>> against the Lord and against his Messiah."
>
> For in this city, in fact, both Herod and Pontius Pilate, with the Gentiles and the peoples of Israel, gathered together against your holy servant Jesus, whom you anointed, to do whatever your hand and your plan had predestined to take place. (Acts 4:24–28)

Note that this prayer presumes a public anointing by the Father of Jesus.

Later in Acts, Peter tells "how God anointed Jesus of Nazareth with the Holy Spirit and with power" (Acts 10:38). We also find in Luke that when Jesus is reading the Isaiah scroll in the synagogue at Nazareth, he is reciting the prophet's prediction of Jesus' anointing:

> The Spirit of the Lord is upon me
>> because he has anointed me
>>> to bring good news to the poor.
> He has sent me to proclaim release to the captives
>> and recovery of sight to the blind,
>>> to let the oppressed go free,
> to proclaim the year of the Lord's favor. (Luke 4:18–19)

Jesus then closes by saying: "Today this Scripture has been fulfilled in your hearing" (4:21). And the baptism of Jesus by John was just reported in the previous chapter.

It is obvious that this anointing of Jesus was so important in early Christian tradition that the title "Christ" became Jesus' last name. Justin Martyr, the philosopher of the second century, in his *Dialogue with Trypho* records this interesting exchange: Trypho the Jew remarks: "For we all expect that Christ will be a man [born] of men, and that Elijah when he comes will anoint him." Justin then explains that "the Spirit of God who was in Elijah preceded as her-ald in [the person of] John, a prophet among your nation; after whom no other prophet appeared among you".[6] Irenaeus, in his *Demonstration of Apostolic Preaching,* refers to two anointings: first, the Father anoints his Son with the Holy Spirit in eternity for all eternity; second, the Father anoints the Lord with the Holy Spirit at the Jordan River in time. While there is a Trinitarian dynamic at work here, Christian understanding of this dynamic does not develop until much later. What is clear, though, is that Jesus is anointed with the Spirit by the Father at his baptism. Note that in later tradition water and oil are linked to the Holy Spirit, and Christ and anointing are linked in baptism. And thereby is fulfilled the coming of the Messiah, the anointed one whom the prophets foretold.

In this baptism at the Jordan, we see the first presentation of the Trinity in the Gospels, with God the Father bestowing the Holy Spirit upon his Son that he may share the power of the Spirit with his followers. The Trinity takes its point of departure from the Son who is introduced to us in his public ministry by his forerunner, John the Baptist. In this, John becomes for us both the gateway to the Gospels and our first witness to the Trinity.

In the last two chapters we have considered the radical new message of a radical reformer who is calling into question some of the foundations of Second Temple Judaism. For this reason, it is crucial to grasp how new John's message is. Therefore, let us review in a brief summary the content of John's startling message—a message that was essential to prepare the way for the Lord.

John proclaimed to the Jews that lineal descent from Abraham would not guarantee salvation (Matthew 3:9), thus removing the basis for any false complacency on their part. The God who had called Israel out of Egypt and led them across the Jordan River was now creating a new people by passing them through the waters of baptism in that same river. The twelve stones that had been set up to mark Israel's crossing of the parted Jordan River (see Joshua 4) would themselves be raised up into twelve new tribes if the people of Israel would not repent. John was attacking the use of religious-ness to resist the demands of God for justice—a theme Jesus would use against the Pharisees.

John's new rite of immersion wiped away the sin of presumption and the whole of one's old life. John, by this washing, was preparing his disciples for the coming tribulation by gathering wheat into God's granary, while the chaff would be burned in unquenchable fire (Matthew 3:12). John was reviving the common Hebrew idea of the last judgment that each one must walk through a river of fire. John's baptism was radically different from Jewish ablutions on many counts. It was not a daily ritual to achieve levitical purity. It was a one-time only transformation to secure forgiveness of sins in anticipation of the coming day of wrath. It required no temple sacrifices, and, unlike circumcision, it was open to all, including women and sinners by profession. It was John, not Jesus, who first opened a way to God for those who, before, had felt themselves excluded. Thus, the crowds who came to John included tax collectors and prostitutes (Matthew 21:32; Luke 3:12; 7:29). The welcome of the excluded was a major source of John's magnetic appeal (as was true, of course, also of later Christianity).

Nowhere in any Jewish source is rebirth made a metaphor for redemption. John's rite was so unique that he was named "the Baptizer." Clearly Jesus regarded John's baptism as given him by God (Mark 11:27–33). John's revolutionary baptism circumvented the temple and alienated the religious authorities. (John's rejection of the priesthood, though he himself was a Levite, may have been due to the widespread revulsion against the corruption of the temple and its priesthood in the first century—a conviction that John and the Essenes both shared.)

Both John and the Essenes also shared an eschatological urgency, expecting an imminent judgment. Both called on Israel to repent, denying that mere Jewishness was enough to save. Both used washings, broke with the temple culture, taught prayer and fasting and focused on Isaiah as their guide to the future. However, John differed from the Qumran community in a number of ways. They wore white linen, but he dressed in homespun, like the poor. His disciples did not settle in a community but wandered around with the itinerant ascetic, as Jesus' disciples would later do, or they would go home and return at various intervals. John required no three-year probation as was the Qumran practice. He accepted anyone who came, provided that they were truly repentant in thought and action. Qumran's ethic applied only to its own community, but John's was addressed to the entire nation. While the Essenes were secretive, exclusive and withdrawn, John was opening salvation to all, even sinners and tax collectors and prostitutes—an openness that scandalized both the Essenes and the temple authorities. John interpreted Isaiah 40:3 to mean that the wilderness was the place for crying out, not a place for escaping society in order to live apart and study Scripture. Qumran expected a prophet and a messiah of Aaron and a messiah of Israel. But John expected a coming figure different from all three: "one who is more powerful than I is coming after me; I am not worthy to carry his sandals" (Matthew 3:11); "He will baptize you with the

Holy Spirit and fire. His winnowing-fork is in his hand" (Luke 3:17), "the Lamb of God who takes away the sin of the world!" (John 1:29).

John emphasizes that humility is crucial both for the precursor and for the follower of Christ. This is essential to the magnificent role stated for John in the Gospel of John. John came that all might believe in Jesus, the light of the world, through John (John 1:7). The Greek here uses the reflexive pronoun, *autos*, himself, to emphasize that it is through John himself that all come to believe. This summary of John's message makes clear the radical newness of the message John preached. He participated in and initiated that mission which Jesus claimed for his own: "See, I am making all things new!" (Revelation 21:5).

## QUESTIONS FOR REFLECTION

- What is the quality that makes John's form of baptism unique? How is John's title, the Baptist, a reflection of that uniqueness?
- How do the four different accounts (in each of the four Gospels) of John's baptism of Jesus embody different details and reflect the problems that the early church had with Jesus being baptized at all?
- How does John's baptism prepare for and lead up to the later Christian baptism? How are the elements of water and the Holy Spirit involved in John's baptism of Jesus?
- How is John's baptism of Jesus the first witness to the Trinity in the Gospels? What qualities of the dove makes that bird an appropriate symbol of the Holy Spirit?

- The word *Christ* means "anointed." How and when was Jesus anointed in the Gospels?

**NOTES**

[1] Josephus, *Life*, p. 1.

[2] Josephus, *Antiquities of the Jews*, XVIII, 5, 2, p. 83.

[3] Adapted from Kurt Aland, ed., *Synopsis of the Four Gospels: Greek-English Edition of the Synopsis Quattuor Evangeliorum* (Stuttgart, Germany: German Bible Society, 1993), p. 16.

[4] Quoted in Charles H. H. Scobie, *John the Baptist* (Philadelphia: Fortress, 1964), p. 148.

[5] Rudolf Bultmann, *The History of the Synoptic Tradition*, John Marsh, trans. (New York: Harper & Row, 1963), p. 252.

[6] Justin Martyr, "Dialogue with Trypho," p. 219.

# CHAPTER FIVE

# The Arrest and Execution of the Last Prophet

"Precious IN THE SIGHT OF THE LORD / IS the death of his faithful ones" (Psalm 116:15). The fate of the prophets in the Old Testament is that they must preach an unwelcome message to an unreceptive audience, and for this they received untold suffering. Matthew's version of the death of John has echoes in his later woes' speech: "Woe to you, scribes and Pharisees, hypocrites! For you build the tombs of the prophets and decorate the graves of the righteous" (Matthew 23:29). Luke in his parallel passage makes this the result of the fulfillment of prophecy:

> Therefore also the Wisdom of God said, "I will send them prophets and apostles, some of whom they will kill and persecute," so that this generation may be charged with the blood of

all the prophets shed since the foundation of the world, from the blood of Abel to the blood of Zechariah, who perished between the altar and the sanctuary. (Luke 11:49–51)

The odd background to this discussion of the killing of the prophets is that there are only two true prophets who are killed in the Old Testament: first, a little-known prophet named Zechariah who lived around 837–800 B.C. (not the post-exilic Zechariah), whose murder by stoning is recounted in 2 Chronicles 24:20–22, and second, the prophet Uriah who was brought back by King Jehoiakim and slaughtered in Jerusalem (Jeremiah 26:20–23). There was also a non-biblical tradition that Isaiah met his death by being sawn in half. But the significant conclusion here, is that, apart from Christ, the major prophet whose killing is recounted in the whole Bible is John the Baptist.

The evangelists are here establishing a parallel between the sufferings and death of the prophet in the Old Testament, the sufferings and death of John and the anticipated suffering and death of Jesus. The ancient axioms are being verified that the prophet must suffer and that "prophets are not without honor except in their own country" (Matthew 13:57). We will see here as we have seen elsewhere: The evangelists go to great lengths to emphasize the correspondences between John and Jesus. Each suffers a passion and an imprisonment before his death. Each is pursued by the Herodian family—Jesus as an infant by King Herod the Great and John by his son Herod Antipas and Antipas's wife, Herodias. Both of these persecutors feared the people more than they feared the prophets. "Though Herod wanted to put him [John the Baptist] to death, he feared the crowd, because they regarded him as a prophet" (Matthew 14:5). Similarly, the chief priests and the Pharisees "wanted to arrest him, but they feared the crowds, because they regarded him [Jesus] as a prophet" (Matthew 21:46). The echoing language reinforces the parallel and makes it unmistakable. Both John and Jesus criticize the authorities publicly and both are prepared to condemn sin wherever it is found and whatever the consequences. John attacks Herod and Herodias for their unlawful marriage while preaching in Herod's territory (Mark 6:17–18); Jesus attacks the Pharisees and the High Priests to their faces throughout the Gospels. It is especially important to note that it is Jesus himself, and not just the evangelists, who points out these parallels. While some might argue that these statements were made by the Gospel writers, rather than being direct quotes of Jesus, these passages are here taken at face value. Two such passages are notable in this regard. First, Jesus draws a contrast in the receptions they receive, a contrast that highlights the similarity in the opposition they generate: "For John came neither eating nor drinking and they say, 'He has a demon'; the Son of Man came eating and drinking, and they say, 'Look, a glutton and a drunkard, a friend of the tax-collectors and sinners!' Yet wisdom is vindicated by her deeds" (Matthew 11:18–19). The second case occurs when, immediately after the Transfiguration, Jesus makes an emphatic parallel of their destinies: "But I tell you that Elijah has already come, and they did not recognize him, but they did to him whatever they pleased. So also the Son of Man is about to suffer at their hands" (Matthew 17:12–13). In this extensive series of parallels, we see that John the Baptist is preparing the way for Jesus, that the evangelists and Jesus himself wish to make this pattern of parallels a clear indication that John was both a prophet of Christ and the first Christian martyr.

One other parallel is instructive as we begin to explore the reasons for John's arrest and execution, and this one lies in the accusation against John that "He has a demon" (Matthew 11:18) reported only once in the Gospels, but then by Jesus himself. There are many times in the Gospels when the same accusation is made about Jesus (Matthew 9:34, 12:24; Mark 3:22; Luke 11:15; John 7:20; 8:48, 52; 10:20). In this culture it seems that a first step in defeating your adversary was to cast him as a demon. The accusation that Jesus reports is based on the fact that John was a desert ascetic given over to extreme fasting and thus, "he came neither eating nor drinking." We should remember that the desert was regarded as the habitat of demons, and it was there that Jesus was tempted three times by Satan.

John's most common location, as reported to us by the Synoptic Gospels, was in the wilderness beyond the Jordan near Jericho. It was a territory rich in religious associations. Here Elijah rode his chariot of fire in a whirlwind up to heaven (2 Kings 2:4–14). Here Joshua crossed the Jordan to enter the promised land (Joshua 1:2–3). Here Theudas, the first-century messianic revolutionary, led his ill-fated assault on Jerusalem (see *Antiquities of the Jews* 20:97–98; Acts 5:36). But the most important facts about this territory in John's time are, first, that the land was part of Perea, a province under the jurisdiction of Herod Antipas, and second, that it was acquiring a reputation as a breeding ground for revolutionaries and brigands.

We have two accounts of the execution of John—one in Josephus, and the other in the Synoptic Gospels, especially Mark and Matthew. If we look first at Josephus's accounts of Machaerus and of John's execution, we will understand the political situation which is not recounted at all in the Gospels. Alarmed by John's growing popularity, Herod feared an uprising. Josephus, in the *Antiquities of the Jews*, describes the motives for John's arrest and execution in these words:

> Herod decided therefore that it would be much better to strike first and be rid of [John] before his work led to an uprising, than to wait for an upheaval, get involved in a difficult situation and see his mistake. Though John, because of Herod's suspicions, was brought in chains to Machaerus, the stronghold that we have previously mentioned, and there put to death, yet the verdict of the Jews was that the destruction visited upon Herod's army was a vindication of John, and God saw fit to inflict such a blow on Herod.[1]

Josephus confirms for us that John attracted large crowds to his desert preaching and that these crowds were profoundly influenced by his words. Herod Antipas's action was a preemptive strike designed to prevent an insurrection. So who was this man, Herod Antipas, and what was the sensitive political situation that caused him to arrest a popular preacher and prophet? He was one of the three sons of Herod the Great who had ordered the slaughter of the innocents in an attempt to kill the baby Jesus. When Herod the Great died, his three sons were given his kingdom by Augustus Caesar. In the division of territory, Herod Antipas became tetrarch of Galilee and Perea. Perea was the territory in which John preached and where presumably, he was arrested. Josephus narrates for us how Antipas married the daughter of Aretas, King of Nabatea, a kingdom of great power that bordered on Perea, so this marriage seemed to be one of political convenience, designed to keep peace between the two kingdoms. However, Antipas went on a visit to Rome where he lodged with a half-brother of his, named Herod, and fell in love with his wife, Herodias (a woman who was also Antipas' niece). Herodias agreed to elope with Antipas but on the condition that he divorce his wife, the Nabatean princess, an action likely to stir up trouble between the two kingdoms of Perea and Nabatea. Antipas's wife got word of this and, feigning ignorance, asked permission to go to the fortress of Machaerus, which bordered on the Nabatean kingdom. She got permission and promptly fled back to her father, King Aretas. It was in the context of this politically volatile situation that John in Mark's account "had been telling Herod, 'It is not lawful for you to have your brother's wife.' And Herodias had a grudge against him, and wanted to kill him" (Mark 6:18–19). This accusation of an unlawful marriage showed a domestic discontent with Antipas which would only encourage King Aretas's opposition in light of Herod

Antipas's divorce of his daughter. Aretas bided his time until A.D. 36 when he invaded Perea and soundly defeated Antipas's army.

This brief synopsis shows that Josephus's account and the Marcan account can easily be reconciled (though some have found them contradictory). In Jewish law, "If a man takes his brother's wife, it is impurity; he has uncovered his brother's nakedness, they shall be childless" (Leviticus 20:21). So John was correct, especially as the brother, Herod, had not died. John's charge then made of Antipas and Herodias public sinners against the law. Thus, John's charge was a politically incendiary one on both domestic and international fronts. John must have known when he made this charge that it would lead to his arrest. Antipas would have no choice but to silence John. To condemn, in effect, Antipas's split with the Nabateans, would be seen by Aretas as subversive activity and would rouse the Jews of Perea against their king.

While John's preaching was moral and not political, it forced Antipas, who Mark tells us "liked to listen to him [John]" and regarded John as "a good and holy man" (Mark 6:20), to place John in a kind of protective custody in the fortress at Machaerus, where John seems to have been imprisoned for a period of time before being executed. During his imprisonment, John seemed to enjoy a measure of freedom in that his disciples could visit him and relay messages, as we will see in the next chapter when we explore Jesus' views of John. The ruins of this magnificent fortress can be seen to this day overlooking the eastern shore of the Dead Sea. Josephus has given us a detailed description of this fortress that Antipas inherited from his father, Herod the Great:

When Herod came to the throne he decided that no place would better repay attention and the strongest fortification, especially in view of the proximity of Arabia; for its situation was most opportune, commanding as it did a view of Arab territory. So he surrounded a large area with walls and towers, and founded a city there, from which an ascent led up to the ridge itself. Not content with that he built a wall round the very summit and erected towers at the corners, each ninety feet high. In the middle of this enclosure he built a palace, breath-taking in the size and beauty of the various rooms; and at carefully chosen spots he constructed a number of tanks to receive rain-water and maintain a constant supply. He might well have been competing with nature in the hope that the impregnability the place had received from her might be outdone by his own artificial defences. He further provided an ample store of weapons and engines, and managed to think of everything that could enable the occupants to snap their fingers at the longest siege.[2]

The death of John the Baptist is recounted for us in all three of the Synoptic Gospels. Although there are significant differences in these accounts, they all agree that John was imprisoned "for the sake of Herodias," though Luke adds "and for all the evil things that Herod had done" (Luke 3:19), though he does not specify what these were. The Herodian family was a cruel and vindictive bunch, and they did not scruple even at killing members of their own family. Herod the Great had set the precedent by killing one of his own wives and three of his sons. Antipas does not put John to death at once, because "he feared the crowd, because they regarded him as a prophet" (Matthew 14:5). It is also recounted that Antipas liked to listen to John. But whatever fear of John or partiality for John that Antipas may have had, his reluctance to execute John was overcome by the cunning and vindictiveness of his wife and his stepdaughter. (Salome, whose name is not mentioned in this account, was a child of Herodias by her prior husband, Herod. Herodias's marriage to Antipas remained childless, as Leviticus predicted for such illicit relationships.) In Mark's account we even get a phrase that implies that Antipas imprisoned John to protect him from Herodias: "And Herodias had a grudge against him, and wanted to kill him. But she could not, for Herod feared John, knowing that he was a righteous and holy man, and he protected him" (Mark 6:19–20).

The word for "protected" here is in the Greek imperfect tense and thus implies a long, repeated action. Antipas knew of Herodias's hate and was trying to restrain it, at least in Mark's account. Mark continues: "But an opportunity came when Herod on his birthday gave a banquet." It is in this dramatic scene that the two women work their conspiracy to kill John the Baptist and to exact their revenge.

No scene in world literature, not even that of Medea killing her children in revenge for her husband's infidelity, can match the unrelenting hatred, the diabolic cunning of this mother and daughter conspiring to avenge the public insults of the prophet. Poor Antipas is completely outmaneuvered by a dancing girl and her mother who find their opportunity in a birthday banquet that

Antipas gives for "his courtiers and officers and for the leaders of Galilee" (Mark 6:21). Excavations of the dining room of the royal fortress show two adjacent but independent rooms, probably one for men and one for women. This would correlate with Mark's account where Herodias is in a different room from Antipas and the banqueters. Some scholars presume that this was a stag party setting in which Salome performs her dance before a room full of half-intoxicated men. Some question whether a princess of the royal house would ever perform an erotic dance in such a context. However, in light of what we know of the low moral standards of the Herodian family, this would not seem unlikely. The part of the story that does require questioning, however, is Antipas's offer of half his kingdom to Salome. Antipas's promise seems preposterous on two counts: First, it is highly unlikely that he would give away half his wealth for any reason; second, the kingdom did not belong to Antipas but to the Romans, and no one knew this better than Antipas. But it makes a good yarn and may be one of those legendary accretions that great yarns acquire as they grow. Matthew in his account even reduces the offer to granting Salome "whatever she might ask" (Matthew 14:7). Herodias seems to exercise an authority over her daughter that compels her to ask for the head of John the Baptist on a platter. Mark tells us of Antipas's reaction: "The king was deeply grieved; yet out of regard for his oaths and for his guests, he did not want to refuse her" (Mark 6:26). What a twisted sense of morality: The man who had no scruples over breaking Jewish law by marrying Herodias and does not hesitate to behead John feels compelled to keep an oath to a dancing girl—an oath that requires the head of the prophet the king was protecting.

The head of John the Baptist, in a scene memorialized in art, is given by Salome to Herodias, and we are left to wonder what disposition she made of her enemy's head. The disciples, we are told, came and took his body and laid it in a tomb. But Herod Antipas must have suffered nightmares about this bloody decapitation for long after. When Antipas hears of the works of Jesus, he says to his servants, "This is John the Baptist; he has been raised from the dead, and for this reason these powers are at work in him" (Matthew 14:2). What a remarkable declaration by a nonobservant Jew to express belief in resurrection from the dead which the Sadduccees denied and which was a late-developing belief for Judaism. How scary must have been the thought of John's return! There is an ancient saying that the just man, like sandalwood, perfumes the blade that cuts him down. Even in his death at the hands of his enemies, and the burial by his disciples and the presumed resurrection in the tortured conscience of Herod Antipas, the evangelists find parallels with Jesus. It is for this reason that the Greek Orthodox Church on the feast of John's death, January 29, sings: "How shall we call you, prophet? Angel, apostle or martyr? Angel because you lived as though without flesh. Apostle because you taught the Gentiles. Martyr because you were decapitated for Christ."

## QUESTIONS FOR REFLECTION

• How do the evangelists point out to us a series of parallels in the destinies and the executions of John and Jesus? Do these parallels justify the verdict that John is the first Christian martyr?

- Where was John's most common location in the wilderness of Judea? Who was the governor of this area and why had it acquired a reputation as a breeding ground for revolutionaries?
- What mix of motives on the part of Herod Antipas and of his wife, Herodias, led to the execution of John the Baptist?
- John the Baptist showed great courage in confronting public sinners and public scandal, even among the rulers of his country. How can we and church leaders today imitate his example?

**NOTES**

[1] Josephus, *Antiquities of the Jews*, XVIII, 5, 2, pp. 83–84.
[2] Josephus, *The Jewish War*, pp. 387–388.

# CHAPTER SIX

# Jesus' Views on His Precursor

WE HAVE DWELT SO FAR MOSTLY ON WHAT JOHN THE Baptist thought of Jesus. But this one-sided emphasis makes all the more urgent and curious the question: What did Jesus think of John? As we embark on this exploration, it is well to remember that while the Baptist's knowledge of Christ was limited but accurate, Jesus' knowledge of John the Baptist was extensive and informed by both his human and his divine understanding. Many of the judgments that Jesus asserts in the passages we will study here extend beyond the reach of human understanding. They call upon Jesus' divine omniscience. The issue of whether Jesus' knowledge was human or divine, limited or omniscient, is a very controversial matter in present-day Christology. My assumption here is that Jesus is portrayed as sometimes having only a human knowledge, e.g., when he did not know who touched him in the crowd

(Mark 5:30–33) or when he did not know when the last day would arrive (Mark 13:32). Sometimes, he is portrayed as having divine knowledge, e.g., when he predicts the exact circumstances of his death (Matthew 20:17–19), or the destruction of the temple (Matthew 24:1–2), or the details marking the end of the world (Matthew 24:3–31), or asserting his own divinity as in "Before Abraham was, I Am" (John 8:58) or "I and the Father are one." (John 10:30). (Some would argue here that these words are John's Christology and not Jesus' own words). My attempt here is not to explore the difficult issue of Jesus' explicit self-understanding but to define how Jesus, the God-man, viewed his precursor, John, from both a human and a divine viewpoint. Only the divine Jesus could declare John the greatest of all those born of woman (Matthew 11:11).

Considering the meager attention the Synoptics generally give to John, it is ironic that two of them, Matthew and Luke (probably using the common hypothetical source Q), give considerable attention (about eighteen verses each) to John's sending of disciples to Christ from his prison cell at Machaerus.

Combined in this passage are two elements that require our closest scrutiny. The first is John's astonishing, mysterious and seemingly tragic question: "Are you the one who is to come, or are we to wait for another?" (Matthew 11:3; Luke 7:19). Seemingly abandoned by God and man, a common feeling of martyrs, John receives no direct answer, but Jesus confers on John an eloquent accolade, the most favorable and extended eulogy that Christ gives to anyone in any of the Gospels.

Second, as we strive to put in context this eulogy of Christ's, we are compelled to notice how rare in the Gospels is Jesus' or the evangelists' praise for any human being. Even the members of Jesus' own family get poor notices in the words of the evangelists. Even Mary seems negatively portrayed when Jesus' family presumably accepts the verdict of the crowd that he is deranged (Mark 3:21) and the verdict of the Jerusalem scribes that Jesus is possessed by demons (Mark 3:21–30). To Peter, Jesus says: "Get behind me, Satan! You are a stumbling-block to me" (Matthew 16:23). Throughout the Gospels, the apostles are consistently portrayed as a slow-witted, uncomprehending group. We can hear the frustration in the Lord's voice: "You of little faith, why are you talking about having no bread? Do you still not perceive?...How could you fail to perceive that I was not speaking about bread?" (Matthew 16:8–9, 11). The disappointment of Jesus is palpable in the repeated questions to his apostles.

Even when Jesus praises someone in the Gospels, it seems grudging praise, as it is quickly countered by disappointment. In the case of the rich young man, the Gospels note that Jesus loved him and that he lacked only one thing—to give his possessions to the poor and then to follow Christ. But the evangelist notes "he went away grieving, for he had many possessions" (Mark 10:17–22). But there are a few occasions when praise is given, though quite reluctantly, as in the case of the Syro-Phoenician woman, who seeks to have Jesus cast the demon out of her daughter. Jesus' first reply is the harsh rebuke that, "it is not fair to take the children's food and throw it to the dogs." But she answered him, "Yes, Lord, yet even the dogs eat the crumbs that fall from their masters' table" And he said to her, "Woman great is your faith! Let it be done for you as you wish" (Matthew 15:26–28). These brief episodes and this fierce reluctance to offer praise set a context and offer a dramatic contrast to the praise that Jesus lavishes on his precursor, John the Baptist.

First, we need to read this whole, extraordinary eighteen-verse passage:

When John heard in prison what the Messiah was doing, he sent word by his disciples and said to him, "Are you the one who is to come, or are we to wait for another?" Jesus answered them, "Go and tell John what you hear and see: the blind receive their sight, the lame walk, the lepers are cleansed, the deaf hear, the dead are raised, and the poor have good news brought to them. And blessed is anyone who takes no offense at me."

As they went away, Jesus began to speak to the crowds about John: "What did you go out into the wilderness to look at? A reed shaken by the wind? What then did you go out to see? Someone dressed in soft robes? Look, those who wear soft robes are in royal palaces. What then did you go out to see? A prophet? Yes, I tell you, and more than a prophet. This is the one about whom it is written,

'See, I am sending my messenger ahead of you,

who will prepare your way before you.'

Truly I tell you, among those born of women no one has arisen greater than John the Baptist; yet the least in the kingdom of heaven is greater than he. From the days of John the Baptist until now the kingdom of heaven has suffered violence, and the violent take it by force. For all the prophets and the law prophesied until John came; and if you are willing to accept it, he is Elijah who is to come. Let anyone with ears listen!

But to what will I compare this generation? It is like children sitting in the market-places and calling to one another,

'We played the flute for you, and you did not dance;

we wailed, and you did not mourn.'

For John came neither eating nor drinking, and they say, 'He has a demon'; the Son of Man came eating and drinking, and they say, 'Look, a glutton and a drunkard, a friend of tax-collectors and sinners!' Yet wisdom is vindicated by her deeds."
(Matthew 11:2–19)

This extraordinary praise, which Jesus offers of his precursor, is so rare in the Gospels that many scholars offer it as evidence of the Christianizing of the Gospels and of John the Baptist by the early church. But let us remember that one of the best attested facts in the New Testament is the baptism of Jesus by John the Baptist. As we have explained, this event was a source of great embarrassment and difficulty to the early church, so it is highly unlikely that they invented this passage in order to adapt John the Baptist to the interests of the early church. The scholars who subscribe to this ungrounded theory do so largely because of the contrast between the Synoptics' treatment of John and that of the Gospel of John. We will consider this more in the next chapter, but here it is essential to note that both sources give great praise to John; the Synoptics praise him as the precursor, and John's Gospel praises him as the faithful witness to Christ.

Now as we look closely at this remarkable passage in Matthew's account, the first puzzle we encounter is the Baptist's question of Jesus: "Are you the one who is to come, or are we to wait for another?" The very question seems to belie and to undermine John's mission. We must recall that John and Jesus have met only once in the Gospel accounts and that was on the occasion when John baptized Jesus. John's personal knowledge of Jesus was accurate but limited, while Jesus' knowledge of John was extensive through his own contact, his disciples' reports and through his divine knowledge and that of the Holy Spirit (though the assertion of this knowledge would not be accepted by many historical scholars). This question is a shocking one because with it John seems to demolish his life's achievements as precursor. It is for this reason that many have regarded it as a rhetorical question or as one that was asked by John on behalf of his disciples. Knowing that his time to pass from this world was drawing ever closer, some theorize that John is attempting to transfer his disciples to Christ. We can find this theory in many of the early fathers of the church, such as Saint John Chrysostom, Saint Augustine, Saint Hilary and Saint Cyril of Alexandria.

Whatever grain of truth there may be in this theory, there is little evidence for it in the text. At least in the Synoptic Gospels, we are never told any of John's disciples become disciples of Christ, though this switch is reported in John's Gospel on the part of

Andrew and perhaps Philip. But it must be noted that this question is never asked, and we must look for the answer and the meaning of this question in the two Gospels where it is asked—in Matthew and in Luke.

Our presumption, and that of the text in Q (the common source of Matthew and Luke), is that the question is a valid one and has its full force for both John and Jesus. Consider John's situation: John is in Herod's prison in Machaerus and faces the relentless hostility of Herodias who is there also. He has lost his ability to continue his mission as the precursor. He is probably very puzzled and troubled by the fact that Jesus has never announced that he is the Messiah. Despite the reports of his own disciples on Jesus' activities (Matthew 11:2; Luke 7:18), John is experiencing doubts about whether Jesus is the Messiah. Perhaps we should say difficulties, as Cardinal Newman has counseled us that "one thousand difficulties do not constitute one doubt" in matters of faith.

We continue to watch how often the evangelists parallel an event of John's life with one in Jesus' life. Here they recount John's personal Gethsemane, his trial by ordeal. Though John was filled with the Holy Spirit throughout his life, this does not remove his tribulations; this does not take away his fear that his mission as precursor is a failure. His abandonment in prison links him with the mystics of Christian tradition who suffered the dark night of the soul and the martyrs who felt abandoned by God and cried out with Christ: "My God, my God, why have you abandoned me?" This trial of faith is the crown and glory of the Baptist, as Jesus himself makes clear later in this passage. But for this to be true, we must take the question seriously as a sign of mental agony, as a trial of everything that John's life stood for. It is not a question of rhetoric, it is a question of suffering.

A clue to the proper interpretation of this question comes to us, as the passage continues. Jesus addresses his answer directly to John the Baptist, albeit through intermediaries, John's disciples. "Go and tell John what you have seen and heard," Jesus says and then lists six signs of the Messiah that are recounted in the Old Testament, Scriptures with which John, being a Levite and a priest, was quite familiar. Five of the six signs which Jesus cites are clear echoes of Isaian prophecies and are seen as such by most scholars. The sixth sign—the curing of lepers—is referred to in the Gospels of Matthew and Luke in a context with strong messianic implications. The references for the six signs are these:

- giving sight to the blind (Isaiah 29:18; 35:5; 42:16–17 and Luke 4:18),
- curing the lame (Isaiah 35:6),
- curing the leprous (Isaiah 35:6; Matthew 10:8; Luke 4:27),
- restoring hearing to the deaf (Isaiah 29:18; 35:6),
- raising the dead (Isaiah 26:19) and
- preaching the good news to the poor (Isaiah 29:19; 61:1; Luke 4:18).

With the citation of these deeds, which John's disciples had witnessed, Jesus is replying to John: Yes, I am the Messiah who was to come, but I have come, not as the fiery political reformer you expected and not as the military conqueror many of the Jewish people expected, but as one who heals and frees and resuscitates, who cares for the unfortunate and who preaches the good news to the poor. I have come as the fulfillment of the prophecies of the prophets.

Jesus is giving John the assurance he is seeking, but with the distinction of roles with regard to John's expectations. Jesus is not publicly proclaiming himself the Messiah, lest he provoke the authorities and compromise his mission. It is a delicate line of diplomacy he must follow in order to accomplish two of his aims: first, to assure John, but second, to maintain the messianic secret—a strategy important to Jesus' mission in each of the Synoptic Gospels. Jesus must conceal his identity from the people and from the authorities until the proper moment. But Jesus' seemingly evasive reply is cleverly couched in prophetic terms that give to John the assurance he seeks.

The question is often raised as to what knowledge John had of Jesus. Here they are conversing at a distance, yet on familiar terms, as if they knew one another personally. But what John specifically does not know about Jesus is whether he is the Messiah the Scriptures predicted. Here Jesus is diplomatically assuring John that he is the Messiah that the prophets longed to see.

At the close of these remarks, Jesus gives what is actually a personal and affirmative response to John: "And blessed is anyone who takes no offense at me" (Matthew 11:6; Luke 7:23). (The word *blessed* here in the original Greek is singular, *makarios*.) Paradoxically, this beatitude seems to be more a warning than blessing. But its praise for John in not losing faith in Christ under his perilous circumstances is confirmed by the immediately following accolade. The two passages together assume that John the precursor will accept Jesus' definition of his role as a Messiah who fulfills prophetic promises, and John will now lose his fear that his life's mission might not be accomplished, and in so doing, he may be able to accept his dark night of the soul as an expression of God's love.

In the next part of this passage, Jesus discusses the nature of the relationship between them, and thus we see Jesus himself expounding the doctrine of John the forerunner to people who knew both John and himself. Jesus testifies to John's character and function at the same time that he testifies to himself as the one who is to come and who has come. Twice in this passage in both Matthew (11:9, 11) and Luke (7:26, 28), Jesus uses the words: "Yes, I tell you," "Amen, I tell you," or simply "I tell you," words which he reserves for his most solemn and significant statements. So what we are hearing in this passage is the authoritative judgment of Jesus, the Word and the Truth. What then does Jesus affirm here in Matthew 11:7–15 and in the parallel passage, Luke 7:24–30? In this passage Jesus is affirming nothing less than the unique role that John the Baptist was filling in salvation history. First, Jesus underscores John's great success in drawing people to his baptisms in the desert. He then defines in a series of rhetorical questions what John was not: a reed shaken by the wind, one dressed in soft robes and living in a royal palace. Scholars have pointed out that Jesus may have with these words been contrasting John with his inveterate enemy, Herod Antipas, whose coins featured a reed and a tetrarch beautifully dressed and living in a royal house.

Jesus then proclaims John a prophet and "more than a prophet" (Matthew 11:9). How are we to understand this curious compliment? He expounds it for us in the next few verses. First, Jesus quotes the prophecy from Malachi 3:1: "See, I am sending my messenger ahead of you, / who will prepare your way before you (Matthew 11:10)." Note that the "you" here is Jesus himself! Jesus is quoting the signature line that defines John as the forerunner, the line that opens the first Gospel written, that of Mark, the line that establishes John as the gateway to the Gospels. So John is, first of all, more than a prophet, because he is the precursor of Christ, a role reserved for only one prophet and a role that was also predicted in the same words by Second Isaiah (40:3–5), where this prophecy ends by proclaiming: "Then, the glory of the LORD shall be revealed, / and all people shall see it together, / for the mouth of the LORD has spoken" (Isaiah 40:5). And the Lord here is speaking in John's place. He is doing the work of the forerunner and saying implicitly that he is the Messiah because John can no longer serve this function as he sits in his prison cell at Machaerus.

Next, Jesus gives us his second reason for declaring John "more than a prophet," and this he precedes with his solemn assurance: "Truly I tell you," a passage he then ends with the urgent warning: "Let anyone with ears listen!" (Matthew 11:15). Rarely in the Gospels does Jesus bracket any message of his with such emphasis. And his message is startling: "Among those born of woman, no one has arisen greater than John the Baptist; yet the least in the kingdom of heaven is greater than he." Jesus is declaring John the greatest of the human race, the model of saintliness (though the Greek was a male form, *gennetois*; implying he is greatest of men). This tribute is the source of the later depiction in Christian art, called the *Deësis* (or supplication) in which Mary and John the Baptist are pictured as the chief intercessors for humankind before the throne of God. (We will discuss the history of this distinctive Christian image in a later chapter.) John's greatness has many roots: His total surrender to the will of God, the presence of the Holy Spirit in him from his birth, his spectacular human achievements in luring all Israel to the desert for baptism and repentance, his defiance of the public scandal of Herod and Herodias, his humility in the service of Christ, and in sacrificially renouncing himself. The forerunner is great both by the highest standards of human achievement and by the norms of spiritual integrity and personal victory over sin. He had earned this most astonishing accolade in the Scriptures.

Yet no sooner is this praise lavished on John than it seems to be retracted: "Yet the least in the kingdom of heaven is greater than he" (Matthew 11:11b). The scholarly controversies over this line and over this whole passage testify to the fact that this is one of the most difficult sayings of Jesus in the Gospels. To understand it properly, one must see this line in its context of the next three verses: "From the days of John the Baptist until now, the kingdom of heaven has suffered violence, and the violent take it by force. For all the prophets and the law prophesied until John came; and if you are willing to accept it, he is Elijah who is to come"

(Matthew 11:12–14). What compounds the problem of interpretation here is that we have a whole passage full of difficult sayings
which are intended to explain the inherent obscurity. It is bewil-
dering to look back at what some of the fathers of the church made
of this passage. Saint John Chrysostom in his "Homily on
Matthew" (36–37) gives a surprising interpretation that was
accepted by a number of both Eastern and Western fathers. He
interprets the "least in the kingdom of heaven" as referring to the
Lord himself(!) on the grounds that Jesus was regarded as obscure
and unimportant to the people surrounding him. But this seems
far-fetched and without a clue in the text. Why would Jesus, after
implicitly declaring himself the Messiah, change and hide himself
in this obscure expression of "the least in the kingdom of heaven"?

An interpretation more firmly based in the text is one that
sees here a comparison of John's record with the least person who
enjoys the supernatural grace of the kingdom of heaven. The two
halves of verse 11, separated by the conjunction "yet," show that
the two halves contradict one another in a typical Semitic method
of phrasing, called a dialectical negation, a method of balancing
two sides of one truth. Jesus is defining the relationship of John the
Baptist to himself and to the kingdom of heaven. He is also marking off two great epochs of prophecy and fulfillment, the law and
the prophets on one side of the boundary and the kingdom of
heaven on the other. John himself is the boundary marker with a
foot in each camp, one foot in the Old Testament and one in the
New, one role as the last prophet of the old order, and a new role
as a precursor and martyr in the new order. John is at once the

beginning of the end of the old era and the end of the beginning of the new era. Some scholars see John as belonging only to the old order as they read this passage because he is not a part of the kingdom of heaven. But Matthew makes it quite clear that John belongs in the era of the inaugurated kingdom when he puts in John's mouth the message of Jesus: "Repent, for the kingdom of heaven has come near" (Matthew 3:2). When he tells us that "all the prophets and the law prophesied until John came," he is telling us that the era of promise and expectation is over and the era of fulfillment begins with John. He is not excluded from the kingdom of heaven, as some would have it, as that would make no theological sense. Both John and Jesus began their preaching ministries with the exact same words: "Repent, for the kingdom has come near." It is at hand with the Incarnation of Christ, though it is fulfilled only with the Redemption and Pentecost. John is the mediator between the Old and the New Testaments precisely because he saw and participated in the fulfillment of the prophecies, and it is for this reason that the church honors John as a Christian apostle and martyr. We must perceive that verses eleven and twelve argue that anyone who enters the kingdom of God ranks higher in privileges than even the greatest person of the old era, but at the same time in this paradoxical Hebrew idiom, the text argues that John is more than a prophet, he is an apostle of the new order of grace who suffers violence for the kingdom of heaven and enters it by his spiritual force. He is the Baptist especially because he baptized the Lord and witnessed the descent of the Holy Spirit upon the God-man's human nature. It is for this reason John is now much more than a prophet, he is the fulfillment of the ancient prophecies of Isaiah and Malachi; he is proclaimer of a new age for which he is himself the boundary marker; he is the mediator of the old and new covenants; he belongs to the period of the realization of the kingdom of heaven, as we are told in Acts 1:22, when this period is defined for us as "beginning from the baptism of John." Note that the whole emphasis in defining the beginning of this crucial period of fulfillment is on John, not Jesus. John's ministry is the turning point of history and John's participation in this ful-fillment was the goal for which all other prophets could only long.

But this comparison defines a relationship between John and anyone who is already in the kingdom of God, between John's supreme dignity in this world and anyone who enjoys a new escha-tological existence in the kingdom of God, whether that is a king-dom created by the death and resurrection of Christ, or the king-dom of God in heaven. Whether that kingdom is in the immediate future, created by Christ's death or whether that kingdom is with Christ in heaven. John stands as the precursor to both kingdoms, and Jesus' balanced statement is an affirmation of the special sta-tus of John and the special status of anyone who enjoys the king-dom of God.

The concluding section of Jesus' discourse on John is a com-parison of the different attitudes people held of John and of him-self. Jesus is contrasting the two views, and to introduce these opposing viewpoints, he uses a parable drawn from popular games of the day and perhaps a popular song. The section is then closed with a saying from the wisdom tradition. It is a short but very distinctive part of the Gospel particularly because it reveals how Jesus' Palestinian contemporaries regarded both him and John.

The abundance of parables in the Synoptic Gospels show us that this was one of Jesus' favorite methods of teaching. The controversies over the meaning of Jesus' parables show us that this literary genre can be interpreted in many different ways. And the shorter it is, the more likely it is to carry a wide range of meanings. Parables are really extended similes or a metaphors and tend to focus on one point of comparison. Drawn from realistic events in ordinary life, they function as a puzzle or a riddle designed to lead the mind of the audience into a surprising or paradoxical insight. They are often dialectical in nature, setting up a dialogue or contrast that leads to a moral statement that is the challenge of the parable. Let's look first at the brief text of this parable:

> But to what will I compare this generation? It is like children sitting in the market-places and calling to one another,
>
>> "We played the flute for you, and you did not dance;
>>
>> we wailed, and you did not mourn."
>
> For John came neither eating nor drinking, and they say, "He has a demon"; the Son of Man came eating and drinking, and they say, "Look, a glutton and a drunkard, a friend of tax-collectors and sinners!" Yet wisdom is vindicated by her deeds. (Matthew 11:16–19)

My interpretation is one of many, but the one that I find most plausible. Jesus introduces his parable with two groups of children who are playing street games. The first group wants to play "wed-

ding," so they pipe a wedding tune, but the second group refuses to
dance. Then the first group switches their tactics and sings a
funeral dirge, but the second group once again refuses to cooperate
by beating their breasts in mourning. (Interestingly, Jesus here
seems to be quoting a popular song of the day.) So this little
vignette gives us the picture of a sulky and capricious group that
wishes neither to rejoice nor to mourn. This contrast of attitudes
with its antithetic parallelism (piping and dancing versus singing a
lament and mourning) sets us up in form and context for the appli-
cation of this typical parable riddle-speech to Jesus' neat contrast
of John with himself.

Jesus then contrasts the people's reception of John with their
reception of himself. Reversing the parable's sequence of joy, then
sorrow, Jesus applies the parable first to John, the ascetic prophet
who even brought his audience to himself in the desert, the traditional haunt of demons. (Remember Jesus' temptations in the
desert by Satan.) As a result, we learn that John's adversaries tried
to demonize him by charging: "He has a demon." In John's Gospel
the Jews also made the same charge against Jesus: "Are we not
right in saying that you are a Samaritan and have a demon?" (John
8:48). This is another of those parallels that come up so often in
the Gospels between Jesus and John. Jesus on the other hand,
comes eating and drinking, and is charged with being "a glutton
and a drunkard, a friend of tax-collectors and sinners." Like the
sulky children of the parable, these critics reject both kinds of missionary strategies—John's tactic of extreme asceticism and Jesus'
tactic of friendly social interaction. Both John and Jesus have

adapted their message to their audience, but always as true prophets of God. But the fierce prophet of repentance is rejected, as is the joyous, social prophet of the kingdom of God.

The passage closes with the wisdom saying: "Yet wisdom is vindicated by her deeds" (or in Luke, "by all her children"). Despite the fact that Israel is rejecting the two final prophets of God, who are joined together here as the prophets of wisdom, God's wisdom and his plan of salvation will finally be acknowledged and accepted through the deeds of Jesus and of the children of wisdom who accept the words of John and Jesus.

In this short, crisp, three-part passage, Jesus has given us his verdict on John the Baptist. He indirectly answers John's question by assuring him that he is the Messiah, while still keeping the messianic secret. He surprisingly asserts that John transcends the category of prophet and is the greatest of humans, apart from Mary. He is the true measure of human wisdom and of human sanctity. He is the boundary marker of the ages, Elijah revived and a man whose wisdom parallels that of the Lord.

## QUESTIONS FOR REFLECTION

- Search the four Gospels for occasions when Jesus offers praise or rebuke to individuals. What conclusions can you draw from this search? Does Jesus offer any accolade to any human being that even approaches his praise of John the Baptist as "greatest among those born of woman"?
- How do you interpret the Baptist's question: "Are you the one who is to come, or are we to wait for another?" As this is a highly

disputed passage, mount the strongest case you can for your interpretation of this question.

- What evidence do we have in Matthew 11:2–19 that Jesus is uttering one of his most solemn and authoritative statements in the Gospels? How does Jesus himself describe the role of his fore-runner?

- Explain how John belongs to the new order of grace and is not excluded by Christ's words that "the least in the kingdom of heaven is greater than he." What parallels with Jesus assure us that John is an important part of the era of grace and of fulfill-ment?

# CHAPTER SEVEN

# John's New Role in the Fourth Gospel: Witness to Christ

The FOURTH GOSPEL, THE GOSPEL OF JOHN, IS A radical departure from the portrayal of John the Baptist in the Synoptic Gospels. The appellation "Baptist" is never used by John the Evangelist. In fact, in the fourth Gospel Jesus is never even baptized by John, although the Trinitarian scene with the Father, the Son and the Holy Spirit is retained in this most Trinitarian of the four Gospels. Instead, the fourth Gospel gives a new definition of John's role: John "came as a witness to testify to the light, so that all might believe through him" (John 1:7). This new and exalted role for John comes ironically in a Gospel that has, as one of its purposes, to moderate and to refute some of the exaggerated claims made by his disciples on behalf of John the Baptist. Only in the fourth Gospel does John the Baptist give an interpretation of himself as not the Messiah, not Elijah and not the prophet. Only in the fourth Gospel are the sayings of the Baptist applied directly to Jesus, as he hails Jesus by a number of significant titles, some of which occur only in the fourth Gospel. An interesting witness, indeed. In this chapter we will probe the meaning of his testimony.

The importance of John the Baptist to the evangelist of the fourth Gospel can be seen in the fact that the majestic prologue that introduces this Gospel is interrupted twice with key references to John the Baptist. The first reference is in the style of a typical opening for historical narrative in the Bible, and then immediately defines the new role that John takes on in this Gospel:

> There was a man sent from God, whose name was John. He came as a witness to testify to the light, so that all might believe through him. He himself was not the light, but he came to testify to the light. The true light which enlightens everyone, was coming into the world. (John 1:6–9)

In the fourth Gospel John is no longer a preacher of repentance and of impending judgment. He is given a new role as a witness to the light, "so that all might believe through him." The emphasis on John as the precursor and as the preparer of the way of Malachi's prophecy (Malachi 3:1) is replaced by an emphasis on John as witness to Israel (John 1:31) and to the whole world.

The historical coming of the Logos, the Word, derives particularly from a messianic passage in Isaiah: "The people who walked in darkness / have seen a great light; / those who lived in a land of deep darkness— / on them the light has shined" (Isaiah 9:2). Thus, the evangelist's favorite image for the work of the incarnate Word, Jesus, is light. And John is to testify to this light so that all—the whole world—may believe. John's testimony then is the gateway to Christ by his witness which stimulates faith in Christ.

One element which gives a different cast to John's Gospel is its polemical background. Even into the second century the disciples of John the Baptist claimed that he, John, was the Messiah and maintained that the Baptist ranked higher than Jesus because he preceded him. The Gospel of John is then often at pains to keep John the Baptist's role in a proper perspective with regard to Jesus. Thus, Jesus here is the true light in contrast to John who is described later in this Gospel by Jesus as "a burning and shining lamp, and you were willing to rejoice for a while in his light" (John 5:35). Jesus is the light, and John is a small reflection of his light.

The second reference in the prologue to John is both significant new testimony and a statement designed to counter any notion that the Baptist might be greater than Jesus because he began his ministry first: "John testified to him and cried out, 'This was he of whom I said, "He who comes after me ranks ahead of me because he was before me"'" (John 1:15).

The significance of this testimony is that John the Baptist confirms the main theme of the prologue, namely the preexistence of the heavenly Word that became flesh. Thus, John as witness guarantees the central tradition of the fourth Gospel, and he defeats any notion that John the Baptist might be greater than Jesus because he began his public ministry first. This theme of preexistence is so important that it is repeated in the first chapter at 1:30 by the Baptist.

In this Gospel the very first disciples follow Jesus as a result of John's witness rather than a call from Jesus. John's Gospel gives special emphasis to faith, and the Baptist is the road to faith that all might believe through him, as we hear both in 1:7 and in 10:40–42. Thus, this Gospel highlights John's power to bring others to faith in Christ. He is the first Christian missionary.

It is because John is the road to faith that we must explore his varied testimonies in this Gospel carefully. On day one of this Gospel, the Jews send priests and Levites from Jerusalem to cross-examine John. (All of John's Gospel is presented in the terms of a legal trial and this is the first cross-examination.) They are trying to probe the identity and the role of the Baptist. As a result, in 1:19–23, John the Baptist gives a startling interpretation of himself as not the Messiah, not Elijah and not the prophet! The fact that these priests were probably sent by the Sanhedrin, or by a clique of the ruling party, "the high priests," is evidence that this preacher of penance from the Jordan had a significant "political" following, despite his strictly religious message, and this caused such unrest in Jerusalem that it required an interrogation.

At a time when messianic hopes were lively and messianic movements dangerous politically, the first key question is whether John is the Messiah (Luke 3:15 records this same concern: "All were questioning in their hearts concerning John, whether he might be the Messiah"). The great crowds that John attracted made him a political force (as Herod Antipas had learned). Jewish tradition, as recorded by the Qumran Essenes, had expectations of three eschatological figures: a prophet, a priestly Messiah and a royal Messiah. John himself was performing in his baptisms an eschatological action. Though second-century disciples of John proclaimed him the Messiah, John in the Gospels, as here, consistently denies that he is the Messiah. In fact, in this passage the use of the Greek pronoun for *I*, *ego*, implies that it is not I, but another in your midst who is the Messiah.

A far more complicated issue arises when John asserts in this fourth Gospel that he is not Elijah because this seems to contradict much (though not all) of the evidence in the Synoptic Gospels, especially Jesus' own statement to his disciples right after the Transfiguration:

And the disciples asked him, "Why, then, do the scribes say that Elijah must come first?" He replied, "Elijah is indeed coming and will restore all things; but I tell you that Elijah has already come, and they did not recognize him, but they did to him whatever they pleased. So also the Son of Man is about to suffer at their hands." Then the disciples understood that he was speaking to them about John the Baptist. (Matthew 17:10–13)

How are we to reconcile this contradiction? First, it is always necessary to respect the integrity of each Gospel. In the fourth Gospel there is no reference to or emphasis upon the prophecy of Malachi

(4:5): "Lo, I will send you the prophet Elijah before the great and terrible day of the LORD comes," though this prophecy receives much attention in the Synoptics (see Matthew 11:7–15; 17:10–13; Mark 6:14–16; Luke 1:17). We must remember that in the fourth Gospel, John the Baptist is not any traditional figure of Jewish expectation—neither baptist, nor precursor. He is, instead, preeminently the witness, a clearly defined role in which he participates in the fulfillment of salvation, for which the other prophets could only long. He is also a preeminent figure of humility, whose swan song in this Gospel is: "For this reason my joy has been fulfilled. He must increase, but I must decrease" (John 3:29–30). It is because of this deep humility that John refuses the role of Elijah. Remember that Elijah was taken up into heaven in a chariot; he even later sent a strange letter from heaven to King Jehoram, recounting the Lord's decision against him (2 Chronicles 21:12–15). And in the New Testament he appears with Moses and Jesus at the Transfiguration. John's Gospel seeks to confine the Baptist's role to that of witness and to establish his great humility, which is not seen as clearly in the Synoptics. It would not have been in John's nature to identify himself with such a great figure of Jewish tradition as Elijah.

A few words, then, on the depiction of the Baptist as Elijah in the Synoptics seem in order here. John the Baptist in the Synoptics wore garments like those of Elijah (Mark 1:6; 2 Kings 1:8). He appeared in the desert exactly where Elijah had disappeared (2 Kings 2:4–11). Zechariah in Luke's opening chapter establishes the theme of John as the forerunner: "He will turn many of the people of Israel to the Lord their God. With the spirit and power of Elijah he will go before him, to turn the hearts of parents to their children, and the disobedient to the wisdom of the righteous, to make ready a people prepared for the Lord." (Luke 1:16–17)

This language echoes that of Malachi 4:5 and presents John not as Elijah himself returned, but as a figure who would, like Elijah, evoke the day of eschatological judgment. Malachi 3:2, 4:1 and Isaiah 48:1 all compare Elijah and his work to a refining fire. In Matthew, John predicts that Jesus will baptize with the Holy Spirit and with fire, and he prophecies that "the chaff he will burn with unquenchable fire." One scholar, J.A.T. Robinson, has even made the ingenious surmise that Jesus' cleansing of the Temple was an implementation of the prophecy and program outlined in Malachi 3:1–4. This is the passage that has the signature line, which John quotes in each of the four Gospels:

> See, I am sending my messenger to prepare the way before me, and the Lord whom you seek will suddenly come to his temple. The messenger of the covenant in whom you delight—indeed, he is coming, says the Lord of hosts. But who can endure the day of his coming, and who can stand when he appears?
>
> For he is like a refiner's fire and like fullers' soap; he will sit as a refiner and purifier of silver, and he will purify the descendants of Levi and refine them like gold and silver, until they present offerings to the Lord in righteousness. Then the offering of Judah and Jerusalem will be pleasing to the Lord as in the days of old and as in former years.

Elijah was the man of fire par excellence in his defeat of the prophets of Baal (1 Kings 18) and in his disappearance in a chariot of fire (2 Kings 2:11). John is the fiery preacher from the desert who forecasts that every tree that does not bear good fruit will be cut down and thrown into the fire. What we can see in this comparison of the Gospel of John with the Synoptics is that there are legitimate but different perspectives in which to view the Baptist. The Baptist as forerunner in the Synoptics takes on the role of Elijah, but in the fourth Gospel, he is the humble witness.

The last puzzling denial in this series of three denials to the priests is John's statement that he is not the prophet (John 1:21); the definite article, "the" which appears in the original Greek, is very important here. John in these three denials is disassociating himself from messianic figures. Various messianic pretenders called themselves "prophets," but Jewish tradition especially expected the rule of a unique prophet, a prophet like Moses, who would meet the expectations generated by the ancient prediction of Deuteronomy, given by Moses: "The LORD your God will raise up for you a prophet like me from among your own people; you shall heed such a prophet" (Deuteronomy 18:15).

This figure is referred to in the Dead Sea Scrolls and is the prophet like Moses, clearly expected here in John's Gospel. So the Baptist is not denying that he was a prophet (Jesus in the Synoptics had called him a prophet and more than a prophet). But he is denying that he is the prophet like Moses of Jewish tradition, who was expected imminently in various Jewish circles of the day.

After the three denials the priests press John for a positive statement about his identity, something to satisfy their Sanhedrin bosses. Here, John himself quotes his signature line from Isaiah 40:3: "I am the voice of one crying out in the wilderness, / make straight the way of the Lord" (John 1:23). But only in the fourth Gospel does John the Baptist apply this line to himself; in the Synoptics it is the evangelists who cite this line. Here, the Baptist is asserting that the desert is the appropriate place for him to begin his eschatological task of witnessing to Christ.

Once the emissaries get their answer to John's identity, they pose a question worthy of the theologically minded and rhetorically hairsplitting Pharisees: If you do not accept any of the traditional eschatological roles, why are you performing the eschatological action of baptizing? The Pharisees, who in the fourth Gospel are the ever-suspicious adversaries of Jesus, had recognized that John's rite of baptism, administered only once, had a special religious significance. It was not like the purifying baths of the Essenes and of the Jews generally. And it was not a baptism of proselytes but a baptism that the whole people were to receive—a rite that must have messianic meaning and, therefore, attracted the Pharisees' attention.

John's reply to their query of "why are you baptizing?" features two elements. First, John points out that he baptizes only with water. This response assumes a distinction between two types of baptism that are common to all four Gospels: John's baptism of water only and then, the later baptism by one coming after John with a Holy Spirit and fire (Matthew 3:11; Luke 3:16). This latter is, of course, Christian baptism. Second, John the Baptist here contrasts his baptism with water with Jesus himself: "Among you stands one whom you do not know; the one who is coming after me; I am not worthy to untie the thong of his sandal" (John 1:26–27). John as witness is pointing out the Messiah hidden from men (just as Peter does in his famous confession in Mark 8:27–30), that same Messiah whom we receive in Christian baptism. In doing this, John points out that he is not worthy enough even to perform for the Lord the service of a slave in untying his thongs. The great humility of John, while emphasized also with this line in the Synoptics, is a special highlight of John as witness.

On the second day of the fourth Gospel, the evangelist has John the witness articulate a series of profound testimonies about Jesus: that Jesus is the lamb of God who takes away the sin of the world, the preexistent one who ranks ahead of John, the one who bestows the Holy Spirit in baptism, and the one who is the Son of God and the chosen one. This astounding and positive witness to Jesus is John's chief role in this Gospel, and he imparts this testimony as a compact and complex Christology. The scope of this brief presentation (John 1:29–34) is breathtaking and has become a source of great controversy because the evangelist has woven later Christian interpretations of Christ into his historical narrative. For this reason, historical critics write this passage off, as they do much of John's Gospel as later theological invention. What they fail to grasp is that the evangelists were not even interested in presenting a purely historical narrative; they adopted a very different literary genre—that of Gospel—in which the narrative is written in the service of faith and develops the seeds of theological proclamation that were contained in the historical narrative. Speaking from his Old Testament theological perspective, John breaks new ground theologically in these startling testimonies.

First, John the witness is the only one in the New Testament to use the exact language of "the Lamb of God who takes away the sin of the world" (1:29). This language implies a new concept of Jesus' death as an expiation for sins—a concept that recurs in Johannine literature (cf. I John 3:5; Revelation 7:14). The imagery of the Lamb, despite much controversy, is, for most commentators, drawn from three sources. In Jewish apocalyptic works and in the book of Revelation, we encounter the figure of a conquering lamb who will crush evil in the world (Revelation 7:17; 17:14). This fits with John's warnings of the coming wrath and his expectation of impending judgment that we find in the Synoptics. The apocalyptic lamb is both a natural image for John and yet a surprising revelation of the mystery of Christ.

Second, the lamb has a kinship with the suffering servant found in the Servant Songs of Isaiah, especially Isaiah 53. In this messianic poem, we hear:

> He was oppressed, and he was afflicted.
>> yet he did not open his mouth;
> like a lamb that is led to the slaughter,
> and like a sheep that before its shearers is silent,
>> so he did not open his mouth. (Isaiah 53:7)

This text is applied to Jesus in Acts 8:32, and the comparison known to the earliest Christians only grows in later Christianity. It is also from this part of Isaiah (40:3) that John derives his signature line of "the voice crying out in the desert."

Third, the paschal lamb, a real lamb sacrificed at the Passover, plays a large role in the fourth Gospel and must be referenced here. Passover symbolism in this Gospel peaks in John 19:14, when Jesus is condemned to death at noon on the day before Passover, the very time when the priests in the Temple began to slay the paschal lambs. By the time John the Evangelist was writing his Gospel in the decade of the nineties, Paul had embedded in Christian tradition the sacrificial notion that "Christ our Passover has been sacrificed" (1 Corinthians 5:7). John the witness has in one pregnant phrase identified Jesus as the one who lifts the collective burden of sin that weighs so heavily on all humankind.

In 1:30, John once again reasserts the preexistence of Jesus. This assertion helps establish the superiority of Jesus above John, so that any conflict between Jesus' disciples and John's disciples can be defused. This affirmation also ties in with a major theme of the fourth Gospel—the descent and ascent back to the Father of the Son of God. In Jewish and Christian tradition, the Messiah was to come forth from concealment (in this case, from heaven) and to reveal himself. John now reveals his mission according to the fourth Gospel: "I came baptizing with water for this reason, that he might be revealed to Israel" (1:31). So John's baptism here has a different meaning than in the Synoptics—it is to make the Messiah known to Israel, the chosen people of God. John baptizes, not with a baptism of repentance, as in the Synoptics, but with a baptism that reveals the one who is to come, the Lamb of God who takes away the sin of the world. In all four Gospels John's baptism is presented to us as a preliminary ritual, as a step toward the baptism with the Holy Spirit and with fire that Christ brings. Here in the fourth Gospel, where no actual baptism of Jesus by John is recorded, we are told of the apocalyptic character of waiting for the one who is to come. And John's role here is to unveil the hidden Messiah. It is John's prerogative as well as his limitation that he is to reveal the Messiah to the Jewish people by his witness.

As John testifies to Christ in 1:32, the evangelist here puts the words that are God the Father's testimony to Jesus in the Synoptics on the lips of John! John understands that the Holy Spirit's descent marks Jesus as the Messiah and the one who is to bestow the Holy Spirit in baptism. As the first Servant Song of Isaiah tells us:

Here is my servant, whom I uphold
my chosen, in whom my soul delights;
I have put my spirit upon him. (Isaiah 42:1)

John's witness is only corroborating that of Yahweh. The natural corollary of this testimony is to verify that Jesus is the Son of God, or, as some manuscripts of this Gospel say, the chosen one (1:34). This language corresponds to that of the Synoptic accounts. "This is my Son the Beloved with whom I am well pleased."

John's testimony in this passage is so exalted that it must be the result of a prophetic illumination for John the prophet. God himself authorizes John's office as witness, and he guarantees the content of his testimony. It was John's special privilege that "I myself have seen and have testified" (1:34). In this Gospel the evangelist has made of John a new figure, one not corresponding to the figures of Jewish expectation, the precursor, or the Synoptic figure of the Baptist. He is a new figure, the witness, who fits the atmosphere of a legal trial so dominant in John's Gospel. In chapter three, when John appears for the last time in this Gospel, he appears as the friend of the bridegroom whose last words are the

Mathias Grünewald captures in his somber crucifixion scene the anachronistic figure of John the Baptist beside the lamb, announcing, "He must increase, I must decrease."

joyful fulfillment of his humility: "He must increase, but I must decrease" (3:30). These words are recorded in the artistic masterpiece of Mathias Grünewald's famous crucifixion scene, which shows John the Baptist pointing to Jesus on the cross. These words stand as the epitaph and the epitome of John the witness.

John's performance of his role as witness moves us and this Gospel to the realm of faith in which the Son of Man comes to lead us to the Father. This realm of faith is beyond the reach of reason or experience. It is an affirmation that the historical reductionists can neither understand nor prevail against. John is an authentic witness not to history but to truth and to faith. John's mission was to arouse faith, but the historical critics do not see this because, in Paul's words "a veil lies over their minds" (2 Corinthians 3:15). John allows us to enter a new order of reality, the life of the Trinity, because he has entered it, experiencing the voice of the Father, the light of the Son and the grace of the Holy Spirit. Remember that the Greek word for witness, *martur*, becomes our word for *martyr*. And John was the witness par excellence to Christ in his life and in his death.

## QUESTIONS FOR REFLECTION

- What qualities make for a good witness? In what ways, then, is John an ideal witness?
- How can we see in the priest's interrogation of John the beginning of the theme of the fourth Gospel as one long trial?
- Why is John's role as witness in the fourth Gospel so different from that in the Synoptics? What are the chief testimonies John gives as witness?

- How do John's testimonies move us beyond history to the realm of faith? What does this tell us about the nature of the literary genre of Gospel in its relation to history?
- How can you witness to Christ in your life that many might believe through you?

# CHAPTER EIGHT

# John the Baptist in Eastern Christian Tradition

**In** THE NEXT TWO CHAPTERS WE WILL CALL UPON CHRISTIAN
tradition to give its witness to John the Baptist. What do the later
witnesses of John, theology, history, liturgy and art have to say
about this heroic Christian figure? These witnesses are a strong
counterbalance to the restricted views of historical biblical critics
who see John only as a son of Second Temple Judaism. These
forces of tradition provide us, first looking backward, with the testimony of humankind upon John the Baptist. Second, looking forward, they demonstrate the impact and varied influences that John
the Baptist exercised on later Christianity. We will divide this survey of John in later tradition into two parts: his influence on
Eastern Christian tradition and his influence on Western

Christian tradition. This division is not merely chronological, as both traditions extend far back in history and both continue to the present day. But each tradition gives its own distinctive witness to John the Baptist. First, it is instructive to survey how John is represented immediately after his death in Josephus, in Acts, in the early apocryphal literature and in the Mandaean tradition. Outside of the New Testament, Josephus is the first to recall the Baptist and to give independent testimony about him. As we noted earlier, Josephus, writing his *Antiquities of the Jews* from Rome around A.D. 90, records that John, "a pious man," performed a baptism different from the other Jewish ritual ablutions in that it required that "the soul had previously been cleansed by righteous conduct," and for this John earned the unique title of the Baptist. The memory of John the Baptist, who died around A.D. 30, remained bright for Josephus in A.D. 90, as he recorded also the death of John and the destruction of Herod's army by Aretas the Nabatean King, an event the Jewish people saw as a punishment from God for Herod.

At about the same time we learn from Luke in Acts that John had founded a movement. He recounts that Apollos though "an eloquent man, well-versed in the scriptures...knew only the baptism of John" (Acts 18:24–25). Apollos, a native of Alexandria, shows then the spread of the Baptist's movement to that second city of the empire. In the next chapter of Acts, Paul finds at Ephesus some disciples of John who had never even heard of the Holy Spirit, as they knew only John's baptism (Acts 19:1–3). In John's Gospel we had seen that some of Jesus' later disciples were first disciples of John, Andrew and probably Philip. This existence of a Baptist movement raises a number of questions: Did all of John's disciples become Christians? How long did John's movement continue? We know from the Gospels that some of John's disciples became Christians, even apostles. A number of legends grew up about John and were recorded in the apocryphal gospels (we will examine these below). John's disciples otherwise disappear in the mist of history, except for one peculiar group, the Mandaeans, who practiced a mysterious religion centered around baptism. They first existed on the banks of the Jordan but today are found only in Iraq and Iran. Missionaries who discovered them in the seventeenth century called them "Christians of Saint John," because of the high esteem they had for John the Baptist. They regarded him as a prophet, and even as the Messiah, though the group is basically anti-Jewish and anti-Christian, perhaps as a result of later Muslim and Gnostic influences. They know of John's baptism (largely in terms of what seems to be New Testament borrowings), but they know nothing of John's martyrdom. Mandaeanism is a syncretistic religion and may have exalted John at a late date when the invading Arabs granted tolerance only to religions that had a prophet and a sacred book. Their literature comes from the eighth century, but their testimony of John amounts to accepting him as a prophet and as the Baptist. In fact, they see John as the last and greatest of the prophets, while Jesus and Moses are depicted as false prophets.

John's continuing influence in later Eastern Christianity shows up in a number of the apocryphal gospels. One of the quaintest and most typical of the legends about John that occur in the apocryphal gospels appears in chapter sixteen of *The Protoevangelium of James* (a work of the second century). Here we find an account of Herod's rage after the Magi have left, and he institutes the massacre of the innocents. Elizabeth flees with the baby John to the "mountains of the Lord" to escape Herod's soldiers. When she finds no place to hide, the mountain divides and receives them, and an angel preserves them. In anger, Herod kills Zechariah at the altar.

In the *Gospel of Nicodemus*, probably a work of the third century, (sometimes referred to as *The Acts of Pilate*), another of the great legends about John is recounted—that of John's descent to hades (or hell) to once again serve as precursor and announce the coming of Christ to the precincts of hell: "And now have I come before his face, and come down to declare unto you that he is at hand to visit us, even the dayspring, the Son of God, coming from on high unto us that sit in darkness and in the shadow of death."[1] This incident of Christian legend will later become a common theme of Christian art.

Thus, John was such a gigantic figure in early Christianity that many legends grew up about him. The Clementine Homilies, for example, even report that Simon Magus, the magician who is reported in Acts 8:9–24 to have practiced his arts in Samaria, was a disciple of John the Baptist. The fourth-century Syrian father, Ephraem, mentions "the disciples of John" who glorify him and claim he is greater than Christ. But no event stirred up more legends than the bizarre history of the relics of John the Baptist. After

John was beheaded, the Gospel of Matthew recounts that "His disciples came and took the body and buried it" (Matthew 14:12). Mark adds that they "laid it in a tomb" (Mark 6:29). Tradition has it that John's remains were buried at Sebaste in Samaria, except for the head which Herodias retained and according to Saint Jerome, she pierced the tongue and the eyes with a needle to satisfy her satanic rage.

John's reputation as a most powerful intercessor must have grown enormously, for Saint Paul of Alexandria tells us that the sick and afflicted came to Sebaste to beg for cures through John's intercession, even when the tomb had been emptied by order of Julian the Apostate. If John's empty tomb was considered a relic and shrine, how much must it have been visited earlier. From A.D. 361–363, Julian the Apostate who had reverted to paganism, became the Roman emperor and launched a virulent campaign against Christianity. While in Antioch, he ordered the removal of the remains of Saint Babylos from the environs of the Temple of Apollo in Daphne. He also ordered the remains of John the Baptist dug up and burned in an attempt to wipe out the veneration of John the Baptist. His effort had the opposite effect, as John's head and remains multiplied until ten churches claimed his head and over sixty laid claim to his bones during the medieval cult of relics. The scene of the burning of John's relics became a popular one in Christian art. The Eastern Orthodox Church now celebrates Saint John the Forerunner with six separate feast days, listed below in the order of the church year that begins on September 1:

- September 23 – Conception of Saint John the Forerunner,
- January 7 – The Commemoration of Saint John the Forerunner (main feast day, immediately after Epiphany on January 6),
- February 24 – First and Second Finding of the Head of Saint John the Forerunner,
- May 25 – Third Finding of the Head of Saint John the Forerunner,
- June 24 – Birth of Saint John the Forerunner, and,
- August 29 – The Beheading of Saint John the Forerunner.

Contrary to this tradition of the findings of the head of John, Theodore the Studite in a sermon on the beheading of John, recounts that "one of his disciples reattached his head to the rest of his body," and this tradition is also represented in Eastern art.

While it is common, particularly in Eastern tradition, to see the forerunner as the true founder of monasticism, as one who puts on the angelic habit and as one whose extremes of self-renunciation lead to glorification, it is difficult to link John to early monasticism. References to him in the literature about Saint Anthony and Pachomius, the first practitioners of monasticism in the deserts of Egypt, are exceedingly rare, but the mentions of John from the fourth century are very significant because he is seen as the spiritual father of the monastic movement. The oldest lives of saints from the Egyptian monks and Athanasius' *Life of Anthony* twice mention John as a teacher of the spiritual life. In *The Life of Pachomius* John is seen as a model for Anthony, along with Elijah and Elisha. The Egyptian monks called themselves sons of John the Baptist. Basil the Great compares the ideal monastery to the desert where John preached penitence to mankind. Gregory of Nyssa in his *On Virginity* remarks that "John is our model." Both Gregory of Nyssa and Gregory of Nazianzen note that Basil had lived and acted like John the Baptist and had his Herod Antipas in the Emperor Valens who persecuted him. The asceticism of the Eastern monks features the characteristics of John's life: extended residence in the desert, extreme fasting, celibacy, prayer, meditation on the Bible and missionary zeal. This mysticism of the desert grew out of the Bible and found precedents in Moses and Elijah, but the first Christian who combines all these elements with apocalyptic preaching and a concern for the world, though he was not of the world, was John the Baptist. John was the patron of Christian asceticism and its outstanding exemplar not only in its primitive stages but also today. His death prefigured that of all Christian martyrs, white or red, whether their witness was made in the desert or on the grid. It is John, with his long index finger pointing out the Lamb of God and saying, "He must increase, but I must decrease," who became the model of hermits. It is for this reason that his image appears often in the churches on Mount Athos, the center of Eastern Orthodox monastic life.

As explained before, the Eastern Orthodox Church today has six feast days in honor of John in its liturgical calendar. This grew from the early honors lavished on John which attest to the wide devotion to him. The commemoration of John's nativity is one of the oldest—if not the oldest—saint's feast, introduced into both Greek and Latin liturgies. The church celebrates John's birth, rather than his death as is commemorated with other saints, because it was at his birth that John was filled with the Holy Spirit. It is in Luke that the angel Gabriel predicts of John to his father Zechariah that "even before his birth he will be filled with the Holy Spirit" (Luke 1:15). This privilege and sign of divine favor accounts for the high position that John enjoys in Eastern tradition (we will enlarge on this later). The second feast of John in the liturgy, the Decollation (or beheading) of John, is almost as old. And the oldest martyrologies even mention a feast of the conception of the precursor on September 24. It became a custom of Saint Saba (A.D. 439–452), a native of Cappadocia who later moved to Jerusalem, to celebrate a double office (as on Our Lord's nativity), a practice later adopted by others. The first office signified the time of the law and the prophets that lasted up to John. This liturgy began at sunset and was chanted without an alleluia. The second office celebrated the opening of the time of grace and was a joyous liturgy in which the singing of the alleluia was held during the night.

The celebration of John's birth on June 24 was done with three Masses: the first in the dead of night commemorated the mission of the precursor, the second at daybreak celebrated the baptism he conferred on Our Lord, and the third mass at three honored the Baptist's sanctity. Just as the evangelists went to great pains to parallel the lives of John and Jesus, so too does the Eastern liturgy attempt to put John's liturgy on a par with Christmas.

Over the years this liturgy led to the popular custom of "Saint John's fires," a custom that spread from east to west. With the setting of the sun on June 24, immense columns of flame arose from every mountaintop and in an instant every village was lit up.

One of the highest honors accorded John in the Eastern liturgy is the invocation of his name both during and after the sanctification of the gifts. John is named before any of the other saints and right after the Mother of God. It is also in his name that the first portion of the third offering of the gifts is made. No other saint is accorded so high a place in the solemnity of the liturgy.

John's reputation among the Eastern fathers was an exalted one. Clement of Alexandria in his *Exhortation to the Heathen* calls John "the voice of the Word." Origen calls him "the Precursor of the Light." But no Father praises John more than Saint John Chrysostom, who called him "the prince of monks," and who recounts that the risen Christ gave John the third heaven as a gift. The apostles see the seven heavens and the singular splendor of the third heaven. The Baptist is depicted as the ferryman who will row human beings to their destination in heaven. Chrysostom even explains that those who remember John in this way will be saved. John is translated to the third heaven, Jesus asserts, "because of the blood he had poured out for me." Thus, John joins Enoch and Elijah in the third heaven and is seen as the new Adam in charge of the new world.

In that curious and unreliable medieval history by Jacob of Voragine, *The Golden Legend,* he quotes Chrysostom extensively, showing that through this Eastern Father the great reputation and honor accorded to John spread to the West. The following extended quotation gives us an expansive view of how Chrysostom exalted Saint John:

Explaining why he was "more than a prophet," Chrysostom says: It belongs to a prophet to receive the gift from God, but does it belong to the prophet to give to God the gift of baptism? A prophet prophesies about God, but does God prophesy about him? All the prophets foretold Christ, but of them nothing was foretold; but he not only prophesied about Christ, but the other prophets prophesied about him. All were bearers of the word, but he was the voice itself; as the voice is nearer to the word, and yet is not the word, so John was nearer to Christ, and yet was not Christ.

John's praiseworthiness is understood from the sanctity of his life, whereof Chrysostom says: "John's conduct made the life of all others to appear blameworthy. So, if thou seest a white garment, thou sayest: This is a very white garment! But if thou layest it upon the snow, it would appear to be soiled, although, in sooth, it is not soiled; so every man appeared unclean when compared to John. Furthermore, his sanctity is proved by a threefold testimony. His first testimony comes from above the heavens, that is, from the Blessed Trinity itself. For the Father calls him an angel, and says of him: "Behold I send my angel, and he shall prepare the way before my face." But angel is the name of an office and not of a nature; and therefore he is called an angel by reason of his office, because he exercised the office of all angels. First, of the Seraphim. Seraphim is interpreted fiery because the Seraphim set us afire, and they themselves burn more ardently with the love of God; and in Ecclesiasticus it is said of John:

"Elias the prophet stood up, as a fire, and his word burnt like a torch"; for he came in the spirit and power of Elias. Second, of the Cherubim. Cherubim is interpreted the fulness of knowledge; and John is called the morning star, because he put an end to the night of ignorance and made a beginning to the light of grace. Third, of the Thrones, whose office is to judge; this John did when he challenged Herod, saying: "It is not lawful for thee to have thy brother's wife." Fourth, of the Dominations, who teach us to rule over subject; and John was loved by his subjects, and feared by kings. Fifth, of the Principalities, who teach us to revere superiors; and John said of himself: "He that is of the earth, of the earth he is, and of the earth he speaketh," and of Christ, "He that cometh from Heaven is above all," and also, "But there shall come one mightier than I, the latchet of whose shoes I am not worthy to loose." Sixth, of the Powers, by whom the harmful powers of the air are restrained. They could not harm him since he was already sanctified, but he shielded us from them when he disposed us to the baptism of penance. Seventh, of the Virtues, by whom miracles are done; and John manifested many miracles in himself. For it is a great miracle to eat wild honey and locusts, and to wear camel's-hair and such like. Eighth, of the Archangels, when he revealed greater things, such as those which regard our Redemption, as when he said: "Behold the Lamb of God." Ninth, of the Angels, when he announced lesser things, such as those which regard daily life, as when he said: "Do penance," and again, "Do violence to no man; neither calumniate any man; and be content with your pay."[2]

Chrysostom reflects the Eastern tradition's emphasis on viewing John as an angel and sets his comments into the context of the nine orders of angels, even though he does not accord to him an angelic nature.

Saint John Chrysostom both reflects and gives us many of the reasons for John's exalted position in the Eastern Christian tradition, a reputation that could be verified also in many of the other Eastern fathers. But there is one non-Christian Eastern source that should surprise us in its praise for John the Baptist, and that is the Koran, which devotes several *suras*, or chapters, to John and venerates him deeply as a prophet, even as one of the greatest of the prophets, and he remains a popular figure to this day in Islam. The Koran, seemingly drawing on the Gospels, recounts John's miraculous birth, his life as an ascetic, the tradition that John never sinned and an account of his death. Mohammed, who wished to place himself in the line of the prophets, makes Abraham, John the Baptist and Jesus the chief progenitors in his line of descent. John had the gift of prophecy, then, for Mohammed and called men to the worship of Allah.

The most significant and exalted praise of John in the Eastern Christian tradition is found in Eastern art. The Greek Orthodox Church venerates John above all saints. This high position is confirmed in the exceptional image called the *Deësis*, a word that means "entreaty" or "supplication." In this image the Lord is represented as the Pantocrator and Judge in royal garments on his throne with the Virgin Mary on his right hand and John the Baptist on his left. They appear as the two primary intercessors for humankind often with hands extended or in prayer as gestures of supplication. We do not know when or where this icon of the Deësis first appeared, but it appeared first in the East and was very widespread throughout the Eastern Church and later in the West. What is astonishing is that John is placed on the same level as Mary, the Mother of God, the Theotokos. After them come the angels and finally the saints. This sacred image appears prominently on the *iconostasis*, or screen of icons that divides the sanctuary from the nave in an Eastern Orthodox Church. It should be noted that the Orthodox icon is a kind of sacrament, a part of the liturgical celebration and a representation of heaven. The saints in their glory continue to pray for this sinful world. And the great audacity of their prayer derives from their union as they pray in the name of the whole church. Their prayer at the Last Judgment for the pardoning of sinners links heaven and earth, the church triumphant and the church militant. It is a dramatic image where mercy and justice meet.

This image embodies the doctrines of Eastern Orthodox theology that held that John had been sanctified in his mother's womb by the Holy Spirit (Luke 1:15) and belonged to an order of grace different from the rest of the human race. Since the Orthodox Church does not believe in the Immaculate Conception, as Roman Catholics do, but claim only that Mary was preserved from committing any actual sin, they thus equate Mary's privilege with John's privilege and present them as equals in iconography. (In the East the Feast of the Conception of John the Baptist, noted above as on September 23, replaces the Western

Feast of the Visitation because it commemorates the sanctification of John the Baptist in his mother's womb.) There is, then, in Eastern tradition, no exemption for either John or Mary from original sin because there is no belief in original sin.

A second mysterious trait that Orthodoxy gives to John is that he is regarded as both an angel and a human being. He is marvelously depicted in an image from Mount Athos as a winged angel carrying a scroll and with his decapitated head on a platter in the bottom corner of the painting! The gospels apply to John the words of the prophet Malachi: "See, I am sending my messenger (*angelos*) to prepare the way before me" (Malachi 3:1). The word for messenger in Greek is the same word from which we get our word *angel*. This Greek word *angelos* can mean either angel or messenger. Very early in Eastern and patristic traditions, the idea surfaced that John was an angel. Origen speculated about whether John might have been an angel and whether he became incarnate, just as the Word did. In other words, John was an incarnate angel announcing the incarnate Word. Saint Basil remarks of John: "By his life which was nothing but a perpetual fast, he seemed by nature to belong to the angels." Ancient hymns call John an angel. His spare diet led many ascetics to praise John for leading a life like the angels. In this way Eastern traditions saw human and angelic natures united in John. One line from the Orthodox liturgy of January 29 proclaims: "Come, people, praise the prophet and the martyr, and the Baptist of the Lord, for he is an angel in the flesh."[3] It is also this dual nature of John—as both man and angel—that gives him his privileged place on a par with Mary in the image of the Deësis.

In his testimonies of Christ, John is truly an evangelist. The Eastern Church says of him: "You are a preacher of Christ, an angel, an apostle." There is a sense in which the Baptist's whole life and teaching can be summed up in his words from John's Gospel: "Behold the Lamb of God who takes away the sin of the world." John is often depicted at the head of the glorious choir of prophets. Like Isaiah, the Old Testament evangelist before him, whose words John often echoes, the Baptist, as the last of the prophets, participates in their role of heralding the Messiah. Artists often parallel David, who was inspired by the Old Law, with John who announces the New Law. One of the most beautiful monuments to the idea of John as an evangelist is the chair of the Bishop Maximian, which is in the chapel of the archbishop's palace in Ravenna. The panel on the front of the chair depicts John

The chair of the Bishop Maximian in Ravenna depicts John the Baptist as the first of the evangelists.

the Baptist as an evangelist in the center of the panel, flanked by two evangelists on each side (John the evangelist as the beardless youth). John is depicted then as the first of the evangelists to announce Christ. In his hand, he holds a disc on which is sculpted John's primary symbol in art—the mystic Lamb. Most scholars believe that this work, which was a gift to the Emperor Otho III by the doge of Venice in the eleventh century, was almost certainly a work of Coptic art from Egypt in the sixth century. If so, this shows that this concept of the Baptist as the first of the evangelists goes far back in Christian tradition, even to the earliest ages of the development of Christian iconography. It may even be that it was created by one of those monks or anchorites who adopted John's lifestyle in the solitary deserts near the banks of the Nile. This elegant work is eloquent testimony of the Eastern Church's esteem for John as the first of the evangelists.

In Eastern tradition, the descent of John and Christ into limbo is not a matter of apocryphal legend (as we saw before in *The Gospel of Nicodemus*). This event is rather a part of sacred tradition and is honored in the many images of the descent into limbo in Eastern art, an image that is often referred to as the *Anastasis*, a word that in Greek means "resurrection." There is a *Guide to the Painting of Mount Athos* that specifies for artists the guidelines for rendering specific images. While this guide was written in the eighteenth century, it records artistic traditions that go back to the eleventh century and earlier. In this work, the artist is directed to picture the Savior taking Adam by his right hand and Eve by his left hand. On the left the forerunner is to be shown pointing to Christ. Surrounding them is a choir of saints and prophets. This image is thus recorded in the mosaics of the monastery of Daphne near Athens and in the Church in Torcello near Venice, works of the eleventh and twelfth centuries—but both in the Eastern tradition. What this image, widely reproduced throughout the East, signifies is that John continues to fulfill in limbo that earthly ministry of his as the forerunner and announcer of Christ. In many of these images, John carries a banner that proclaims: *Vidi Salvatorem* ("I have seen the Savior"). The artist is making his claim that this role is the permanent mission of John in Christian history.

In Jewish tradition, though John the Baptist is revered as a prophet in the Gospels and was a great religious figure in the view of Josephus, he was almost completely removed from later Jewish tradition because of his connection with Christ. Even today the *Encyclopedia Judaica* gives a short account of John's life, but denies him the title of prophet. David Flusser, a professor of New Testament at the Hebrew University in Jerusalem, has revived a favorable portrayal of John as a Jewish hero. Another event that has stimulated Jewish reassessment of John is the recent discovery of a cave that is presumed to be one used by John for the immersion of his followers. Shimon Gibson, a British archaeologist, argues that the wall carvings and cleansing jugs, plus its location near Ain Karim, John's hometown, suggest that the cave was used by John.[4] The theory is hotly disputed, but it has served to rekindle Jewish interest in John.

This short review of John the Baptist's stature in Eastern traditions demonstrates why he was accorded a uniquely elevated position. The proof that John was held in such high regard is perhaps best illustrated in the consensus of the three early religions—Christianity, Islam and Mandaeanism—all of which regarded John as a great prophet—No other figure in history has achieved such ecumenical acclaim, except Abraham.

## QUESTIONS FOR REFLECTION

• Why is it significant that three different religions have each given John the title of prophet? What was the role of the prophet in the Old Testament? Does John even today serve as a prophetic spokesman for God?

• Eastern art accords John a most exalted position. How can this high position be demonstrated and interpreted by the image called the Deësis?

• Two later accounts about John tell us much about how Eastern traditions esteemed John. The first, a legend, recounts how an angel hid John and Elizabeth in a mountain, so John could escape the sword of Herod's army, though it then fell on his father Zechariah. The second, an oral tradition, depicted John as the precursor to Christ in announcing his coming to hell or limbo. What parallels to Christ do each of these two stories establish, and why are these significant? How does John the Baptist function as a precursor to Christ for us today?

## NOTES

[1] *The Apocryphal New Testament*, M.R. James, trans. (Oxford: Clarendon, 1924), p. 125.

[2] Jacobus de Voragine, *The Golden Legend* (New York: Arno Press, 1969), pp. 324–325.

[3] Bulgakov, *The Friend of the Bridegroom*, p. 130.

[4] Shimon Gibson, *The Cave of John the Baptist: The Stunning Archaeological Discovery That Has Redefined Christian History* (New York: Doubleday, 2004), pp. 1–4, 211–213.

# CHAPTER NINE

# John the Baptist in Western Christian Tradition

Though JOHN THE BAPTIST WAS VENERATED
in both the East and the West, the ways in which each tradition
expressed this veneration differed widely. In surveying John's place
in Western Christian tradition, we will examine the testimonies of
Western liturgies, of the Western fathers, of Western monastic tradition, Western art and Western popular culture.

The honors paid early and widely to John the Baptist in
Western liturgy attest their singular devotion to him. The commemoration of John's nativity is one of the oldest, if not the oldest feast, introduced into both Greek and Latin liturgies to honor
a saint. Unlike other saints who were honored with a feast on the
day of their death, John is first honored on the day of his birth
because it was then that he was, as the angel Gabriel predicted,

"filled with the Holy Spirit" (Luke 1:15). Only three persons are honored in the liturgy with a feast on their nativity: Jesus, Mary and John the Baptist—the only three to be spared from original sin. While this exemption from original sin is somewhat controversial in the case of John, patristic tradition maintains that John was freed from original sin and sanctified in his mother's womb. This testimony comes from Ambrose, Maximus of Turin, Peter Chrysologus, Gregory the Great and Bernard of Clairvaux. This public veneration of John the Baptist is attested strongly from the fourth century (as in the eleven sermons of Augustine on John the Baptist). The Council of Agde (A.D. 506), presided over by Caesarius of Arles, ranked the nativity of John the Baptist among the greatest of feasts.

In the seventh century the feast of the Baptist's Decollation (or Beheading) enters the Roman liturgy for August 29. The only other people to have two feasts in their honor in the Roman calendar are Jesus, Mary, Peter, Paul and Joseph. This early and exalted positioning of John in the Roman liturgy suggests that John may be the first person to have been awarded the title of saint, though this is difficult to establish definitively. But this may have been the case due to the fact that John is the first person in the New Testament to show Jesus the extreme and unambiguous reverence and awe worthy of God, when he proclaimed: "I am not worthy to untie the thong of his sandal" (John 1:27).

Other elements of the liturgy pinpoint how exalted was the conception of John. In the canon of the Latin Mass (*Nobis quoque peccatoribus*), John was at the beginning of the list of martyrs, as he is today in Eucharistic Prayer I: "For ourselves, too, we ask some share in the fellowship of your apostles and martyrs, with John the Baptist, Stephen, Matthias, Barnabas, Ignatius." The hymn for Lauds on June 24 gives John the threefold crown of prophet, virgin and martyr. Those who wish to see Stephen as the protomartyr of the church argue that John lived before the death and resurrection of Christ and, therefore, cannot qualify. Their view is opposed by the testimony of the liturgy. In the Preface of John the Baptist on June 24, the liturgy proclaims: "You found John worthy of a martyr's death, his last and greatest act of witness to your Son." An ancient Latin maxim of the church, *lex orandi, lex credendi* (the law of prayer is the law of belief), confirms that church tradition is a firm witness to the fact that John is both a Christian saint and a Christian martyr.

One of the earliest indisputable witnesses of the cult of John the Baptist in the West can be found in the baptistery of "the Mother of all churches," St. John Lateran, the first and greatest of the Roman basilicas. In A.D. 313, the Emperor Constantine I gave Pope Miltiades a palace at the Lateran for a papal residence. Originally known as the Church of the Savior, it was rebuilt and rededicated to John the Baptist in 905. Its official and full title is "Patriarchal Basilica of the Most Holy Savior and of St. John the Baptist at the Lateran." But the baptistery of the Lateran, which was constructed in the time of Constantine, shows how ancient is the veneration of John. The *Liber Pontificalis* has a notice in the words of Pope Sylvester (314–335) that on the edge of the baptismal font there stands a statue of John linked with one of the

Savior. Between the two a lamb is represented from whom comes a stream of water. John holds a placard that announces: "Behold the lamb of God." This ancient Christian baptistery sets the precedent for the many Christian baptisteries to be built in later ages.

In the Mass of the Middle Ages, the confiteor, or general confession of sins at the foot of the altar, was recited up to the time of the Second Vatican Council. This solemn prayer established a hierarchy among the greatest of saints:

> I confess to almighty God, to blessed Mary ever Virgin, to blessed Michael the Archangel, to blessed John the Baptist, to the Holy Apostles, Peter and Paul, and to you brethren, that I have sinned exceedingly in thought, word and deed.

The establishment of hierarchies in such prayers may seem trivial to some, but they were always the result of careful theological consideration, as another useful example demonstrates. In the late nineteenth century the question arose whether Saint Joseph or Saint John the Baptist should receive precedence in the Litany of the Saints. In 1869 the Consultor for the Congregation for Sacred Rites, Jerome Saccheri, O.P., agreed with Pope Benedict III, who in 1726 felt that Saint Joseph's name could not precede John the Baptist's in the Litany of the Saints because "to prefer Saint Joseph to the Precursor would have meant more excellent holiness and dignity in Joseph whereas Christ's own words declared of John: 'none greater born of woman.'" Though the issue was decided in the Baptist's favor, some theologians prefer Saint Joseph on grounds that it is more to be father and ruler of Christ than to be

his herald and forerunner. Some would even posit a prenatal sanctification for Saint Joseph, such as Jeremiah and John the Baptist
enjoyed. But in Christian tradition the only one clearly sanctified
in the womb is John the Baptist (apart from Mary).

The testimonies of the Western fathers to John are very rich
indeed. They see John as we have sought to portray him, and as the
opening of Mark's Gospel describes John "as the beginning of the
Gospel of Jesus Christ." They probe the sources for the veneration
of John, and I will try to summarize their views of John around five
central themes. First, they often pursue an understanding of Jesus'
great accolade that none born of woman is greater than John
(Matthew 11:11). For them, John surpasses great prophets in manifesting the Word Incarnate by jumping in his mother's womb and
testifying to the divinity of Jesus as his precursor. Saint Jerome
argues that Jesus calls John an angel, then adds that "the least in
the kingdom of heaven is greater than he."

> Now His meaning is: John is greater than all men, and if you
> want to know, he is even an angel; nevertheless, he who is an
> angel [messenger] on earth is the very least in the kingdom of
> heaven, that is, he is of a lesser rank than the angels. Moreover,
> he who is a minor in the kingdom of heaven, that is, an angel, is
> greater than he who is greater than all men on earth.[1]

Saint Augustine notes that John was so great that he was taken for
Christ. Augustine resolves a long-standing controversy making
saints of both Old Testament figures and John the Baptist:

From this John and afterwards, all those things concerning Christ began to become past or present which by all the righteous men of the previous time were believed, hoped for, desired as future. Therefore, the faith is the same as well in those who, although not yet in name, were in fact previously Christians, as in those who not only are so but are also called so. And in both there is the same grace by the Holy Spirit.[2]

Augustine's summary view of John was this: "If you want to know what perfection man can attain to, it is John."[3] Many fathers call John "the voice of the Word," especially Augustine in his "Sermon on the Birth of Saint John the Baptist." Pseudo-Bernard and Jerome call him "the first of evangelists." Jerome remarks that, "the gospel of the kingdom of heaven is first preached in the Gospel by John the Baptist....Read the Gospels. John the Baptist cries out in the desert: 'Repent for the kingdom of heaven is at hand.' "[4] Origen, Saint Ambrose, Saint Jerome, Saint Leo the Great and Saint Bernard all confirm that John was endowed with prenatal grace and thus was freed from original sin before his birth. For Pseudo-Bernard and Peter Chrysologus, he was the perfection of angelic purity.

A second theme that the fathers develop is that John is the bridge between the Old Testament and the New Testament, between the law and grace. Tertullian, in his commentary on Luke, argues that John marks a break between the old and new order in the economy of salvation. Up until John, he maintains there was only the burdens of the law and no remedies. The yoke of works had been abolished but not the laws.

Saint Basil of Seleucia proclaims that "It is for the whole Church that John was a herald."[5] He is seen as an heir of the desert of the Exodus, a carrier of the hopes of the Old Testament, and then, as the Baptist and missionary who leads us all to be Christians in the realm of grace. Saint Ambrose expresses this well: "There is neither penance without grace nor grace without penance, for penance should first condemn the sin so that grace can do away with it. John fulfilled the type of the Law and baptized to penance; Christ to grace."[6] To the fathers, John is the initiator of the gospel economy and the mediator of things old and new— this is his function as the bridge between the old world of the law and the new world of grace.

A third theme that the fathers illuminate is that of John's baptism as the dividing point of two eras. This Augustine calls the partition between law and gospel. For Augustine, John's baptism is a baptism of repentance, for with repentance, the old life comes to an end, and the new life begins. So for Augustine, with John the Old Testament ends and the New Testament begins. To the fathers, John was the first to recognize the provisional and relative character of his baptism. The fathers question the efficacy of John's rite, asking whether it came from heaven or from earth. Tertullian concluded that it is divine in its institution but not in its effect. For Augustine in his *Enchiridion*, it is not a rebirth in faith, hope and charity. Saint Jerome in a more nuanced view underlines the value of John's baptism by arguing that it derives from its relation to Christian baptism. John's baptism, he maintains, does not forgive sins, but is only a baptism of repentance for the remission of sins later forgiven by the blood of Christ."[10] The efficacy of the sacrament is later established through the passion and resurrection of Christ.

John's baptism of Christ is the occasion for the first revelation of the Trinity and a scene that has won close attention from the fathers and doctors of the church. Saint Ambrose in his "Commentary on Luke" says that Jesus allowed himself to be baptized to sanctify the waters and to give them the power to cleanse away the sins of men. This theory seems far-fetched, but this subject has stirred some strange theories. Saint Augustine and Saint Thomas Aquinas argue that Jesus shortly after his baptism instituted the holy sacrament of baptism, which he administered first to his disciples and then to the people. Their scriptural warrant for this comes from John's Gospel: "As the Scripture has said, 'Out of the believer's heart shall flow rivers of living water.' Now he said this about the Spirit, which believers in him were to receive, for as yet there was no Spirit, because Jesus was not yet glorified" (John 7:38–39). All these theories seem shaped to accommodate the delayed effect of Johannine baptism.

The amazement that the fathers exhibit toward this mystery of John's baptism of Christ is best captured by Pseudo-Bernard:

> The heavens quake, the earth is stunned, the Jordan rejoices, and the angels are astonished that the hands of him who baptizes are holding the Lord of Hosts. What art thou doing, John? Thou hast the boldness to hold with unveiled hands the One whom the Cherubim and Seraphim are almost afraid to even gaze upon? The Angels long to contemplate Him...and thou art not afraid?[8]

Saint Jerome sums up the scene in these words: Christ "is purified by John in the flesh, but He purifies John in the spirit."[9] This mystery which occurs at or near the beginning of each Gospel marks the first and only adult meeting of Jesus and John in the Gospels, and the fathers seem to sense that it is on Jesus' authority that John enters the Gospel and performs his vital functions of baptist and precursor. There is a sense that the kingdom of heaven is suffering violence and a new epoch in the history of salvation, the era of the kingdom of God, has begun.

A fourth theme that runs through the patristic tradition is John's mission. In Luke's words, it was "to make ready a people prepared for the Lord" (Luke 1:17). John's role was to teach the people to recognize and to welcome "the Lamb who takes away the sin of the world." He accustoms the eyes of the people to the glare of the light of the world. John, for Augustine, is not the one who illuminates the world but the lamp that reflects the source. For Augustine, John was sent by God to reveal his great humility, for it is with this virtue that he wishes to equip his people for God. John names himself "the Voice" of one crying out in the desert, make straight the paths of the Lord. It is in this signature saying of John's that the fathers find his significance in preparing the perfect people for the Lord. He is the symbol of all the voices of the prophets that preceded him. In Augustine's "Sermon on the Birth of John the Baptist," from which these thoughts are culled, he makes the point that it is necessary that all the old voices diminish, as one advances in the knowledge of Christ. The more we discover the wisdom of Christ, the less the Voice is needed. The

Voice then gradually ceases its office in the measure that the soul progresses toward Christ. "He must increase, but I must decrease." John's humility is the virtue for which John is exalted by God, the virtue by which he prepares a perfect people for the Lord.

The last theme that the fathers emphasize is our need to imitate John's asceticism. It is not for monks alone but for all the faithful. Before being the place of penitence, the desert is the site for meeting God. It is the haven of solitude and silence. Ambrose remarks that John was "the teacher of abstinence and, as it were, a new angel on earth."[10] He is the patron of solitude and for the fathers, only solitude and contemplation give birth to the Word of God in our hearts. John's desert teacher was the Holy Spirit, and he was truly "taught by God." The Word of God we recall came to John in the desert (Luke 3:2). Bede the Venerable, commenting on this verse, explains, "The desert is the Church, which later, like the barren woman of the psalms and prophets, will rejoice over her numerous children."[11]

Saint Jerome reflects on John's trip to the desert, "John the Baptist had a saintly mother and his father was a priest; but neither his mother's love nor his father's wealth could prevail upon him to live in his parents' house at the risk of his chastity. He took up his abode in the desert, and desiring only to see Christ refused to look at anything else."[12] Jerome's remarks remind us of Christ's words: "He that loves father or mother more than me is unworthy of me" (Matthew 10:37).

John lived in the desert to fulfill the prophecy of Isaiah as "the voice of one crying out in the desert." Before John ever preached, he practiced a long and austere penance. He learned that some

devils are cast out only by prayer and fasting. He learned that mas-
tery of self is the fruit of long, continual and severe self-denial.

This short sketch of the fathers' views of John has barely
skimmed the surface of what we have been given: eleven sermons
of Saint Augustine; twelve by Maximus; commentary by the four
great Eastern fathers: Chrysostom, Basil, Gregory of Nyssa and
Gregory of Nazianzen; and by the five great Western fathers:
Jerome, Ambrose, Augustine, Leo and Gregory. Later saints who
praise John include Bernard, Thomas Aquinas, Peter Chrysologus,
Peter Canisius and Francis de Sales. Few saints in history have
enjoyed so much praise by so many fathers and doctors of the
church. They praise John as the sower of the gospel, the voice of
the apostles, the witness of the Lord, the trumpet of heaven, herald of Christ, gate of life, voice of the Word, preparer of the people for salvation, precursor of the truth. In a work once attributed
to Saint Bonaventure, the *Meditations on the Life of Christ,* the
author confers on John a series of honors:

> He is a patriarch, the chief and last of the patriarchs, a prophet
> and more than a prophet, an angel, but an angel of election; an
> apostle, the first and the prince of apostles, an evangelist and the
> first announcer of the gospel...the voice who cries out in the
> desert, the precursor of the Judge, the herald of the Word; he is
> Elijah and the law and the prophets cease with him...he has
> been elevated to the supreme rank of the Seraphim.[13]

What other Christian figure, beyond Christ and Mary, has had
such praise lavished upon him? What stands out from this survey

is John's enduring role in the church. He is the voice crying out to all peoples. He is the missionary for Christ to the world.

In the New Testament, John the Baptist is the only figure who is a model of the ascetic life. This consideration gave John his unique place in Western monasticism. Jerome in his Epistles repeatedly refers to John as the true founder of monasticism. The *cingulum*, or monastic belt, was modeled on John's "leather belt" (Mark 1:6) and served as a symbol of chastity. John's desert life laid the groundwork for the three monastic vows of poverty, chastity and obedience. Paulinus of Nola wrote a poem of three hundred verses to John the Baptist in which he, too, saw the monastery as reproducing the desert of John the Baptist.

An early problem surfaced when the question was raised: Was the way of John the Baptist also the way of Jesus Christ? Some argued no on the grounds of Jesus' own comparison that portrays John as a fasting ascetic and himself as a sociable "friend of tax-collectors and sinners." But the role of the monks was vindicated by the apostolicity of John the Baptist. He was, as he is described in the prologue of John's Gospel "a man sent from God...as a witness to the light, so that all might believe through him" (John 1:6, 7). The monks saw themselves as descendants of "the first Apostle" and being poor themselves, they were beloved by the poor.

A man's influence is measured by the repercussions of his life and ideas beyond his death. Apart from Christ's temptations in the desert, John's presence and teachings are the only New Testament evidence of a great ascetic and the only gospel foundation we have for a monastic movement that later grows to such huge proportions. Jerome declared to Eustochium: "The founder of the system was Paul, and Antony made it famous: going back, the first example was given by John the Baptist."[14] Is it not amazing that a desert ascetic whose ministry lasted for what was probably only one to two years led to the development of a worldwide monasticism?

As in the case of monasticism itself, so in the case of John, the question was asked: Did John's death to the world signify a refusal to live in the world? And the response, of course, is no. John preached to soldiers, to tax collectors, to prostitutes. He roamed the precincts of the Jordan River to bestow his baptism on as many as he could—a social and communal act. John attracted to his ministry as many as thirty disciples, according to the Pseudo-Clementine literature[15] and these he presumably sent back to their tasks in the world. There is no evidence that John ever set up a monastery like that of the Essenes at Qumran. He was rather an anchorite or hermit who moved freely from his solitary desert hermitage to a site where he would preach to the assembled crowds.

Jerome, in his Homily on the Gospel of John, advises monks: "Realize your nobility, monks! John is the first one of our calling. He is a monk."[16] And in his Homily on the Baptism of Christ he proclaims: Christ "is purified by John in the flesh, but He purifies John in the spirit."[17] By the sixth century, Gregory of Tours is recommending John the Baptist as the model for bishops, most of whom lived like monks. And many monks who lived ascetic lives like John were called to be popes.

Throughout history John has been a patron saint of many religious orders, especially the Carmelites, Augustinians, the

Carthusians and the Franciscans. The Carmelites laid claim to the most ancient order, founded by the prophet Elijah, who it was said imposed upon himself a severe ascetic rule. With the coming of the Christian era, John the Baptist whom they claimed as one of their order, revitalized the Order of Carmel by his words and his example, according to their traditions. The Augustinians inherited their high estimate of John from Saint Augustine who, as we recounted before, found the peak of human perfection in John. The Carthusians have long divided their devotion between Saint John, the patron of ascetics, and Saint Bruno, the founder of the Carthusian order. The Franciscans have a long tradition of esteem for John. For this brief account I would like to convey some of the modern Franciscan devotion to John by quoting a letter from Father Jeremy Harrington, O.F.M., a former provincial of the Province of Saint John the Baptist:

> Our province of Saint John the Baptist took its name from Archbishop John the Baptist Purcell. In the 1840s he traveled Europe recruiting clergy and religious to come to minister to the people in his diocese. Our Franciscan founders came from Tyrol—Innsbruck and northern Italy, which was then Austria. As their first parish the bishop gave them Saint John the Baptist parish in a heavily Catholic, German immigration area. In a very few years when they became independent from Tyrol, the friars took Saint John the Baptist as their patron. A dozen years ago when we started a new friary, we named it John the Baptist. We have various statues of him and reflect on John the Baptist and his spirit but do not have special devotions or rituals. Twenty

years ago I was in Bahia, Brazil, in June for a Franciscan meeting. I was surprised at what a public event, feast and holiday June 24, the Birth of John the Baptist, was there. They celebrated the feast much more than we do.[18]

Our account of John is all too brief to do justice to his stature in Western monasticism. But from the diverse sources we have cited, one can hear the choirs of monks from the fourth to the twenty-first century chanting the praises of this prince of monks.

John, as a subject for Western art, has offered artists a rich opportunity to portray him as the last of the prophets and as the first of martyrs, as archangel or as man but always as a saint, as baptist or as precursor, as ascetic or as priest. This last pairing is of special historical interest. The ascetic image of John dominates Eastern art portraying him with bare feet, emaciated, clothed in his camel hair shirt with his leather belt, with long hair and a bushy beard. The sacerdotal image is prominent in the West, presenting John in long flowing robes, wearing sandals and often carrying a book or a lamb or both. In the East the Council of Trullo in 690 forbade the representation of Christ under the figure of a lamb. So in Eastern art the cross often replaces the lamb, as the staff of the hermit becomes a cross. The sacerdotal image of the West may derive from the emphasis in some of the Western fathers on John as a priest. In one of Jerome's homilies on the beginning of the Gospel of Mark, he outlines this concept:

Just as the apostles set the example for the priesthood, so John the Baptist set the example for monks. As far as tradition goes in the writings of the Hebrews and in the memory of this very day, John's name appears among the names of the priests and of the chief priests.... [M]oreover...his privilege [was not] fittingly allotted except to the foremost of the priests, that is, to the chief priests. Now, why have I said all this? That we may know that this was a chief priest who knew that Christ was to come.[19]

Jerome and Western art seem to perceive John as in his short ministry a mediator between God and humans, a role not inconsistent with his portrayal as an intercessor for humankind in the images of the Deësis.

There is a richness and éclat to the portrayals of John in Western iconography that is surpassed among the saints only by that of Mary. From the fourth century to the seventeenth, John the Baptist was a most popular image. Apart from thousands of individual images, John's life lent itself to great narrative cycles, so much so that he must have set a record with at least forty-six(!) narrative cycles of his life in the West (eight in Florence alone) in a great diversity of artistic forms: miniatures, mosaics, frescos, bas-reliefs, icons, stained glass, paintings, sculptures. The artists who created these cycles were the great medieval and Renaissance masters: Giotto, Andrea Pisano, Ghirlandaio, Ghiberti, Pollaiuolo, Andrea del Sarto, Filippo Lippi, Tiepolo. The cycles, like the famous doors of the Baptistery of the Duomo in Florence, include episodes from both the canonical Gospels and the apocryphal gospels. Some of the unusual images included in these cycles that would run twenty to thirty images are these: The naming of John, the circumcision of the precursor, John preaching to the birds,

John introducing Christ to his hearers, John rebuking Herod and Herodias. One of the most touching and unusual images shows an angel carrying the young John into the desert. Clearly the imaginations of the greatest of Western artists spent much time meditating on the life of John.

John is one of the very few saints to appear in art as both an infant and an adult. His images go back to the beginning of the second century, where the earliest image of John appears in the Roman Catacomb of Saint Callistus, the baptism of Christ. The oldest known example of the Deësis is also in Rome, in the church of Santa Maria Antigua, dated to the seventh century (although older images of the Deësis probably existed in the East). In this unusual version of the Deësis, there is an emphasis on the prerogative of the three freed from original sin. In the center are Jesus and the Virgin Mary, to the right are Saint Anne and Mary, to the left are Elizabeth and John.

In the thirteenth century, interest in John the Baptist received a great stimulus from Dante, who in Canto XXXII of his *Paradiso* presents John the Baptist as seated on the opposite side of the heavenly court from Mary,

> ...ever there to dwell,
>> Who, ever holy, endured the desert's fare
>> And martyrdom, and then two years in Hell.[20]

Dante is presenting a literary version of the Deësis, noting John's "ever holy" status as exempt from original sin, and noting his two-year stay in hell (his expression for the abode of the dead before Christ opened the doors to heaven) before he could announce the

Christ to those in limbo. Honorarius of Autun in the twelfth century had proclaimed John as "greatest of all the saints, equal to the

angels and an angel himself." These two different literary accolades furthered artistic interest in John. Fra Angelico pictures John as the head of the choir of prophets from the Old Testament. In the northern portal of Chartres Cathedral, John is pictured as the greatest and last of the prophets. Lucca della Robbia in the sacristy of the Cathedral of Florence has John seated opposite Mary (as in Dante) but at the head

Fra Angelica's *Choir of Prophets*

of the double college of four evangelists and four doctors of the Latin Church. Like Saint Michael, John is often venerated even in the West as both archangel and as saint. He is even elevated to the dignity of the Seraphim by the fathers and artists of the West. In medieval angelology, the Seraphim were the first of the nine orders of angels. The cult of John the Baptist under all these influences spread rapidly all over Europe. Eight churches in Rome were named for John the Baptist as well as churches in Amiens, Venice, Lyon, Bretagne, Saissons and Chartres. Baptisteries all over the continent were named after John. In fact, this was so prevalent in France, that John was often called Saint John of the Fountains, or Saint John in the Round because of the circular plan of French Baptisteries.

Albrecht Dürer's *The Adoration of the Trinity* contains a Western version of the Dëisis image, with John leading a choir of prophets and saints on the right, and Mary leading a choir of virgins and saints on the left.

In this detail from *The Adoration of the Mystic Lamb* of Van Eyck, we see another Western version of the Dëisis, with Mary and John interceding for mankind.

Van der Weyden's *Last Judgment* is a Deësis image with John the Baptist and Mary as equal intercessors before the Lord.

El Greco's *The Burial of Count Orgaz* shows John in his traditional leather garment, again beseeching the Lord along with Mary for those below.

The greatest artists of the Renaissance continued this popular devotion to John. Albrecht Dürer at the start of the sixteenth century in his *Adoration of the Trinity* places John at the head of the choir of prophets and beside Moses and David. Van Eyck's *The Adoration of the Mystic Lamb* shows John's head surrounded by an inscription that proclaims him as equal to the angels. Van der Weyden in his *The Last Judgment* and El Greco in his *The Burial of Count Orgaz* create Western versions of the Deësis image. Grünewald's Isenheim altarpiece with its crucifixion scene modeled on the Gospel of John memorializes the image of John the Baptist as a prophet who assists in the realization of what he announces. Grünewald's image embodies many of the traditions surrounding John: precursor who points to Christ on the cross and says, "He must increase, but I must decrease," and has beside him those two symbols so characteristic of John—the lamb and the cross. From this glorious peak, the tradition of John in art then declines as the work of secularization gradually suppresses religious symbols and leads Rembrandt to make of John a philosopher and Rodin to depict John as an itinerant ascetic and preacher. Luther's emphasis on faith alone, and particularly his denigration of fasting and ascetic practices, served to turn attention away from John the Baptist in later Western art.

Last in John's position in Western culture, we will take note of his position in popular culture, a little-noticed aspect of John's popularity. A puzzling aspect of Catholic devotion to the saints is the mystery of how certain saints become patrons of different professions. John the Baptist provides a rich array of examples. He is surprisingly and amusingly the patron saint of tailors because he dressed himself in the desert with the garb of a camel-hair shirt and a leather belt. This has endeared him to all dealers in skins: furriers, belt-makers, curriers and even dermatologists. His affection for the lamb has made him the patron of wool combers and cloth merchants. He is the patron of those who catch and train birds either because he was "caged" in prison for a time or because he first witnessed the appearance of the dove at Christ's baptism. Because of his imprisonment and the method of his death, he is the patron of prisoners, of those condemned to die and of cutlers and sword makers. Because of his decapitation, he is the healer of those who suffer from migraine headaches and from diseases of the throat. He is a patron of singers and musicians because Guido of Arezzo, a Benedictine monk, made a hymn in John's honor, using the notes of the scale. He is a healer of Saint Vitus's dance thanks to Salome and her performance, and he is the healer of epilepsy, often called Saint John's sickness because of the legend about the punishment meted out to Herodias who seized the head of the martyr from the silver dish and then fell down, convulsed with rage, foaming at the mouth, and crying out that her soul was damned. (The marvelous theatre inherent in the story of Herodias and Salome should remind us of Oscar Wilde's *Salome* written in 1893, and the 1905 Richard Strauss opera of the same name.)

Devotion to John has led to churches, abbeys, towns, cities, dioceses and religious families being placed under the patronage of John. Among the cities are Calletorto, Florence, Genoa, Ragura, Sarrano, Torino, and Umbria in Italy; Cornwall, England; Quebec,

p 154 Mohammed placed himself
in the line of the prophets
including Abraham, John the Baptist
& Jesus.

p 151 "Liturgy" is man-made
and may apply to an
individual or a group - it
means "how he (or they) worship.

p 154 re Eastern tradition

Numbers 6 re Nazarite vow
6:22-24 = "The Priestly Blessing"?

Bob Braubach 3/1/17

John the Baptist

Chapter 8, p 143
pp 143, 144 Josephus is probably the
most accurate historian outside
of the Bible itself

"Mandeans" are Christian.
Muslim mix - sometime
(combination of different religions)
Only found in Iraq and Iran.

"History creates truth" whereas
Mohamed claimed to be
the Prophet

Canada and San Juan, Puerto Rico. French Canada has national celebrations on the feasts of Saint John. American dioceses that take John for their patron are the dioceses of Charleston, South Carolina; Dodge City, Kansas; Paterson, New Jersey; Portland, Maine and Savannah, Georgia.

The largest Catholic university in the United States, Saint John's in Queens, New York, is named after John and carries the motto, *Ecce Agnus* ("Behold the Lamb") on its crest of arms. The Spanish heritage in the United States is devoted to John in many ways, from the California Missions to the historic Juan Bautista de Anza Trail in Arizona, to the great popularity of the Puerto Rican Santo, San Juan Bautista. One last testimony to the devotion to John in popular religious culture worldwide is that there are at least seventeen saints and blesseds whose full names include the name of John the Baptist. Two of the most prominent of these are Saint John Baptist de la Salle, founder of the Christian Brothers, and the Curé of Ars, whose name in French is Saint Jean-Marie-Baptiste Vianney. Thus, the name of John the Baptist is around the world on the land, in the culture and in the churches. And the great popularity of the name John over the centuries is the product of devotion to John the Baptist.

In the last two chapters we have, looking backward, surveyed the testimony of Christian liturgy, art, monasticism, the fathers and popular culture on John the Baptist. We have found that they constitute a chorus of voices proclaiming John a prophet of three religions, Christianity, Islam and Mandaeanism, the last of the Old Testament prophets and the first of Christian martyrs. He is seen as an angel, literally in the East and more metaphorically in the

West, one freed in the womb from original sin, equal to Mary as an intercessor for humankind, first of evangelists and permanently the precursor. Looking forward, we have seen John as the patron of Christian asceticism and the prince of monks, the initiator of the new order of grace, the teacher of humility, repentance, prayer and fasting, the shaper of a desert spirituality that is needed by all, patron of thousands of baptisteries, churches, cities and professions, and as the guide to Christ who teaches us that he is "the Lamb who takes away the sin of the world." This testimony of tradition stands out in vivid contrast to the view of historical biblical scholars who see John only as a son of Second Temple Judaism.

## QUESTIONS FOR REFLECTION

- What evidence does the liturgy offer us to confirm John the Baptist's status as a celebrated Christian saint and martyr?
- The Western fathers of the church had a rich and varied understanding of John the Baptist. What insights of theirs impress you the most, especially as a contribution to your own spirituality?
- What has John's heritage been in Western monasticism?
- What different aspects of John are imaged in the work of Western artists? How does the testimony of the artists agree with the testimony of the fathers of the church?
- What testimonies to John are found in popular culture?

## NOTES

[1] Jerome, "Homily 16," in *The Fathers of the Church*, volume forty-eight (Washington, D.C.: Catholic University Press, 1965), p. 125.

[2] Augustine, "Letter Against the Pelagians" (III, 11).

[3] Rétif, p. 96.

[4] Jerome, "Against the Pelagians," in *The Fathers of the Church*, volume fifty-three, p. 276.

[5] Basil of Seleucia, STR V, 8, 55, quoted in Rétif, p. 18.

[6] Ambrose, "Letters," in *The Fathers of the Church* (New York: Fathers of the Church, 1954), p. 470.

[7] Tertullian, "On Baptism," 10, in The *Ante-Nicene Fathers*, volume three, pp. 673-674.

[8] Pseudo-Bernard, *Patrologia Latina*, 184, 998, quoted in Rétif, p. 71.

[9] Jerome, "Homily 89," in *The Fathers of the Church*, volume fifty-seven, p. 229.

[10] Ambrose, "Letters," p. 331.

[11] Bede the Venerable, quoted in Rétif, p. 39.

[12] Jerome, epistle 125, *Select Letters of Saint Jerome*, F.A. Wright, trans. (Cambridge, Mass.: Harvard University Press, 1954), p. 409.

[13] John of Caulibus, *Meditations on the Life of Christ* (Asheville, N.C.: Pegasus Press, 1997), p. 105.

[14] Jerome, epistles 22, 36, *Select Letters of Saint Jerome*, p. 143.

[15] Pseudo-Clementine, Homilies 2, 23, in *The Ante-Nicene Fathers*, volume eight, p. 233.

[16] Jerome, "Homily 87," in *The Fathers of the Church*, volume fifty-seven, p. 213.

[17] Jerome, "Homily 89," in *The Fathers of the Church*, volume fifty-seven, p. 229.

[18] Jeremy Harrington, O.F.M., personal letter to the author.

[19] Jerome "Homily 75," in *The Fathers of the Church*, volume fifty-seven, p. 124.

[20] Dante, *The Portable Dante*, Laurence Binyon, trans. (New York: Viking, 1953), p. 534.

# CHAPTER TEN

# John the Baptist: Forerunner Yet Follower of Christ

It IS THE PARADOX OF JOHN THE BAPTIST THAT HE IS BOTH THE forerunner and the follower of Christ. What is in dispute about this statement is the second half of the paradox—John as follower of Christ. The easier portion of this paradox—John as forerunner of Christ—we have explored in some depth with earlier presentations of John as the fulfillment of the prophets, especially Isaiah and Malachi, the proclaimer of the long-awaited Messiah whose role was prophesied by the angel Gabriel and as one who was steeled for his task by the apostolate of the desert. The harder part and the larger focus of this chapter is confirming John as a follower of Christ. In doing this we will pull together some ideas explored earlier, and we will draw on both Gospel and outside-the-Gospel sources.

It is important to define first just what is in dispute. Many historical critical biblical scholars, in their relentless "quest for the historical John" see him as primarily a son of Second Temple Judaism. For them, he is an Old Testament figure who must be judged only on historical criteria. He is for them also one who has been distorted in the Gospels by what they see as the late Christianizing of the Gospels by the evangelists who wrote thirty-five to seventy years after the appearance of John and the death of Christ. The point of view of these historical scholars is one that views the Gospels solely as documents of Enlightenment history and disregards their status as Gospel, as kerygma, as proclamations of faith. John P. Meier, a noted Catholic exegete of the historical Jesus, points out the strange consequences of this viewpoint: "[I]n the quest for historical Jesus, 'the rules of the game' allow no appeal to what is known or held by faith...faith cannot function as evidence or argument in the narrowly restricted confines of Jesus-of-history research."[1] This position leads such scholars to consider as historical a statement such as Paul Hollenback's that faith has blinded exegetes from the obvious insight that Jesus sought baptism from John because, like all the other candidates, he thought himself a sinner. While accepting for consideration this supposedly historical statement, they deny faith-based statements of Christian theologians, such as Charles Scobie's attempt to interpret theologically Jesus' reason for being baptized by John:

Jesus has been thought of as undergoing baptism in order to con-
secrate the sacrament and provide the example for Christians to
follow; or his repentance has been thought of as not being on his
own behalf, but on behalf of others; or his submission has been
thought of as part of his complete self-identification with sinners.[2]

In short, historical speculation, no matter how far-fetched, is
acceptable, but theological speculation, no matter how insightful,
is not. The historian is unwilling to accept faith-based statements
about a faith-based document. The historian would have the rest
of us live within the confines of their narrow perspective.

The distorted viewpoint that these historical critical scholars
bring to a study of John the Baptist and the Gospels is their conviction that John the Baptist and his message have been changed
or "Christianized" in a way that contradicts their purely historical
reading of the Gospels. However, one of the insights of historical
scholarship of the last three centuries is that no history is objective. Every historian brings to his subject his own biases.
Remembering this, let's examine the case for and against the
Christianizing of John and his message.

Those who argue that the Gospels have Christianized John
maintain that he was by birth and training an Old Testament figure, schooled in Second Temple Judaism, but thirty or forty years
after his death, the evangelists put a Christian message on his lips.
To see the true John the Baptist before the emergence of
Christianity, they argue that we must look to Josephus's account of
the true John. Luke's infancy narrative must be dismissed for them

as pure legend without any outside supporting evidence. The Gospels, especially John's Gospel, they charge, set out to reverse a supposed subordination of Jesus to John. Statements such as John 1:15, 30, which testify to the preexistence of Christ, are evidence of the way in which the evangelists altered history to make John conform to the beliefs of later Christianity.

The labors of many historians in questioning the authenticity of the Gospels are vast, but even according to one of its most able practitioners, E.P. Sanders, it has not been fruitful. "Scholars have not," he contends, "and in my judgment, will not agree on the authenticity of the sayings material, either in whole or in part...the enormous labor which for generations has been expended on the investigation of teaching material in the gospels has not yielded a convincing historical depiction of Jesus."[3] This conviction, however, has not deterred Sanders or others from their quest for the historical Jesus or the historical John.

Now let us examine the arguments against the Christianizing of John's message. Without strong positive evidence, the historians contradict the role and message of John, as recorded in five sources—the four Gospels and Acts. Eyewitnesses to John would have still been alive to deny any attempts to deprive John of his role and message or to make of these more than was warranted by his life. The charge of Christianizing comes two thousand years later and is the product of unsubstantiated hypotheses. Even the Josephus account makes of John a pious man who establishes a new kind of ritual washing and whom the Jewish people saw as a servant of God who used the Nabatean armies to punish Herod

Antipas. It was only by preaching a new route to salvation—
"Repent, for the kingdom of heaven has come near"—that John
attracted such huge crowds that he became for Herod a political
liability. To make John only a son of Second Temple Judaism is to
deny the validity of the prophecies of Isaiah and Malachi, to
reduce John to a minor desert ascetic like Bannus and to deprive
him of his role as precursor and baptist. The supposed subordination of Jesus to John finds no support in the Synoptic Gospels and
in John's Gospel, where this charge is presumed to be found, the
evangelist gives to John the exalted status of witness to Christ "so
that all might believe through him." This hardly sounds like the
work of an evangelist eager to downgrade John. The most com-
pelling argument against the historical reductionists lies in the
embarrassing episode of the baptism of Christ. The most memo-
rable event in John's short ministry was his baptism of Christ. By
the historical critics' own standards, an event embarrassing to
Christianity is likely to be true. John's role is so deeply rooted in
each of the Gospels that one must posit an independent conspiracy to Christianize John on the part of each of the four evangelists. The hermeneutics of suspicion practiced by the historical critical scholars cannot overcome the hermeneutics of the text. One
cannot give greater credence to hypotheses than is given to the
text. The wide areas of agreement between Jesus and John and the
high esteem in which Jesus held John are conclusive arguments
against this charge of a later Christianizing.

But there is at work in the Gospels a process of drawing parallels between Jesus and John. Contrary to a secular charge of a

Christianizing of the Gospels, this style of presentation is one that is calculated to bring out the parallels between Jesus and John that were inherent in the events, the teachings and the language of Jesus and John. The point of noticing and emphasizing these parallels is to convince the reader that John, despite being his forerunner, was also a follower of Christ.

At this point, it would be helpful for the reader to remember or review all the parallel elements that were set out in chapter two between the accounts of the birth of John the Baptist and the birth of Jesus, especially the prophecies of the angel Gabriel in both cases, the role of the Holy Spirit and the parallels between the two prayers, the Benedictus of Zechariah and the Magnificat of Mary. We are prepared there to see Jesus and John as partners in the work of salvation—John in announcing the Savior and preparing a people for the Lord, and Jesus as "the mighty savior...in the house of his servant, David." This intricate process of parallelization begins in the infancy narratives of Luke and extends through all the Gospels.

Let us look at the parallels in the events of their lives, then in their teachings and often extending even to identical language. First, the events:

- Both were written of by Isaiah (John in Matthew 3:3; Jesus in Luke 4:17–19).
- Both undergo a spiritual initiation in the desert (John in Matthew 3:14; Jesus in Matthew 4:1–11).
- Both are unmarried and are itinerant preachers (John in Matthew 3:1–12; Jesus in Matthew 5—7).

- Both preached harshly against the scribes, the Pharisees and the Sadducees (John in Matthew 3:7–10; Jesus in Matthew 23).

- Both Jesus and John are portrayed as messengers from God, rejected by their own generation (Jesus and John in Matthew 11:16–19).

- Tax collectors and prostitutes come to both for forgiveness (John in Luke 3:12; Matthew 21:31–32; Mark 2:5–16; Jesus in Matthew 9:10–11).

- John and Jesus are both baptizers (John 3:22–23; although John 4:12 seems to retract that Jesus was baptizing and substitutes his disciples).

- John fasts and Jesus' disciples are later to fast (Luke 5:33–35).

- Both John and Jesus are questioned regarding their identity (John in Luke 3:15; John 1:19–22; Jesus in Matthew 26:63).

- Herod Antipas arrests and kills John the Baptist and intends to arrest and kill Jesus (John in Matthew 14:1–12; Jesus in Luke 13:31–33).

- Both John and Jesus reprove those in authority (John in Luke 3:19; Matthew 14:3–5; Jesus in Matthew 23).

- Both preached the good news (John in Luke 3:18; Jesus in Luke 4:43).

- Both are executed in a horrible death at the hands of political authorities (John in Matthew 14:1–12; Jesus in Passion accounts of all four Gospels).

- The death of each is viewed later as the killing of a prophet (John in Mark 11:32; Luke 9:7–9; Jesus in Matthew 21:11, 46; Luke 24:19–20).

- Both were buried by their disciples (John in Matthew 14:12; Jesus in Matthew 27:55–66; Mark 15:40–47; Luke 23:49–56; John 19:28–42).

In addition to this paralleling of events, there is also a strong similarity in the teachings of John and Jesus:

- Both warn of a false complacency in relying on Abraham as their father as the claim to salvation (John in Matthew 3:9; Luke 3:8; Jesus in John 8:33–39).
- Both preach the urgency of repentance, even using the very same words: "Repent, for the kingdom of heaven has come near" (John in Matthew 3:2; Jesus in Matthew 4:17).
- Both excoriate the Scribes and the Pharisees with the same epithet: "you brood of vipers" (John 3:7; Luke 3:7; Jesus in Matthew 12:34; 23:33).
- Both emphasize the test of deeds and again with the same language and imagery: "The ax is lying at the root of the trees; every tree therefore that does not bear good fruit is cut down and thrown into the fire" (John in Matthew 3:10; Luke 3:9; Jesus in Matthew 7:19; 15:13).
- Both encourage the sharing of tunics as the work of social justice (John in Luke 3:11; Jesus in Matthew 5:40).
- Both emphasize the separation of the righteous from the unrighteous—John with the theme of the wheat and the chaff; Jesus with the parable of the wheat and the tares (John in Matthew 3:12; Luke 3:17; Jesus in Matthew 13:24–30, 36–43).
- The disciples of both John and Jesus are taught to pray and to fast (John in Luke 5:33–39; Jesus in Luke 11:1).

- Both preach the close relation of judgment to righteousness (John in Matthew 3:7–10; Jesus in Matthew 5—7, the Sermon on the Mount).

- Both envision the coming of apocalyptic trials (John 3:12; Jesus in Matthew chapter 24).

- Both preach the caring for the poor and the avoidance of greed (John 3:11–14; Jesus in Luke 16:19–31).

- Both preached against the Temple (John by his priestly silence and avoidance of temple sacrifice; Jesus in John 4:20–24).

- Both preached a more rigorous ethic than the Torah (John because he preached not the religion of the Temple nor the moral code of the Torah, but a person, the Messiah, Jesus Christ; Jesus in Matthew 5:21–48, where Jesus raises the ethical bar above the Torah to "Be perfect, therefore, as your heavenly Father is perfect").

What is the meaning and intent of this extensive array of parallels in events and in teachings? They are, I believe, intended to establish an identity between the precursor and Christ. The evangelists are establishing John in the best Christian sense as an *alter Christus*, another Christ, one who imitates Christ in poverty, chastity and obedience, one who follows Christ in his life and in his teachings. This elaborate set of parallels defeats the notion of those who refuse to allow John the august titles of saint and martyr because the reign of grace and its gifts had not begun. For Scripture tells us that the kingdom of God is at hand when John first and then Jesus, enter on to the scene. The kingdom is "at hand" with the Incarnation but is fulfilled with the redemption and Pentecost. John is the peak of Old Testament saintliness. He is celebrated in the New Testament as the fulfillment of prophecy, as both prophet and apostle, the mediator between the old order and the new grace. John was closer to the Holy Trinity than any other human being. He heard the Father's voice, witnessed the Holy Spirit as a dove and baptized the Christ.

It is no wonder that not only the Gospels but Christian tradition as well bestow the titles of saint and martyr on John. We have seen that Eastern and Western liturgies, Eastern and Western monasticism and Eastern and Western art all agree in conferring these titles on John. Let us remember that these same traditions also confer these titles on the Holy Innocents, who were martyred long before John. (Their feast is kept in the West on December 28.) Jesus' own praise of John and his status as friend of the Bridegroom, model of renunciation and humility, all confirm his right to these titles.

But there are other considerations that we should keep in mind. The evangelists place John at the center of this central period in salvation history. But because he dies before Christ, he must endure what no other Christian has ever endured. He must die a martyr's death without having before his eyes the example of Christ's death, which has steeled every Christian martyr to the sacrifice of his life. John had to die without this motivation but with his deep faith in the Messiah, the Bridegroom for whom he gave his life, as the motive for his martyrdom.

Perhaps the highest compliment given to John in the

Scriptures, after the accolade from Jesus, is the fact that so great is John that he is taken repeatedly for the Christ. In Luke 3:15 we find the people questioning whether John might be the Messiah. In John 1:20, when the priests and Levites from Jerusalem question John, he says, "I am not the Messiah." Most dramatically in Matthew 14:1–2, after Herod Antipas hears reports about Jesus, he says to his servants, "This is John the Baptist; he has been raised from the dead, and for this reason these powers are at work in him." How ironic that this wonderful tribute to John comes from his executioner! It is the ambition of every Christian to show forth the radiance of Christ. In one of his eloquent prayers, John Henry Newman prays, "Let them look up and see no longer me but only Jesus." It is with this subtle indirection that the Scriptures confirm for us that John was an apostle of the imitation of Christ.

Christian theologians have wrestled with this issue of the sanctity of John by theories about his baptism. Saint John of Damascus, for example, maintains that, "John was baptized when he placed his hand upon the divine head of the Lord. He was also baptized in his own blood."[4] Orthodox theologian Sergius Bulgakov holds that

> John's martyrdom is a baptism with blood, but one that took place *before* Golgotha and the Pentecost. This baptism could acquire its full power only in the world beyond the grave, after Christ's descent into hell and after the Pentecost.[5]

But the testimony to John's sanctity that most touches the heart is the crucifixion of Grünewald, where John stands pointing out the crucified Savior, book in hand, lamb and cross and chalice at his side and his statement above his finger, "He must increase, but I must decrease." Could there be any more eloquent testimony by Christians than this to the enduring sanctity of John? The image has stamped indelibly on the memory of Christians the conviction that John, in his way, penetrated to the depths the mystery of the cross.

The value of something to us can often best be measured by considering what would be the effects of its absence. So let us ask, what if there had been no John the Baptist? This question is close also to asking what if John had been only a son of Second Temple Judaism? There would have been, then, the failure of the prophecies of Isaiah and of Malachi. There would have been no prior preparation of a people of God for Jesus. Jesus would have had to prepare his own people, his own way, and announce his own coming. A key Christian witness and martyr would be lost to us. Christians would be without their second major intercessor before Christ after Mary, as depicted in Christian art, and the greatest man born of woman, as described by Jesus. The model of desert asceticism, as seen in the Gospels and early Christianity, would not be there as an example to us and to twenty centuries of Christian monks. We would be poorer for the loss of the rich parallels between Jesus and John. The third most prominent figure in the Gospels, besides Christ and after Peter and Paul, would not be there to enrich our understanding of Christ. We would have Gospels without a gateway.

## QUESTIONS FOR REFLECTION

- Do you think the figure of John the Baptist and his message were later changed and Christianized by the evangelists? Why or why not?

- Which parallels between John and Jesus are most persuasive for you in establishing that John was a follower of Jesus? Are there any arguments that hold weight with you that would deny John the right to be called a Christian saint and martyr?

- What reasons in your mind account for the fact that John the Baptist is repeatedly taken to be the Messiah; to be Christ in the Gospels?

## NOTES

[1] John P. Meier, A Marginal Jew: Rethinking the Historical Jesus, volume two (New York: Doubleday, 1994), p. 112.

[2] Scobie, p. 148.

[3] E.P. Sanders, Jesus and Judaism, (Philadelphia: Fortress, 1985), pp. 4, 5.

[4] John of Damascus, "Writings," in The Fathers of the Church, p. 348.

[5] Bulgakov, The Friend of the Bridegroom, p. 75.

# John as Model for Contemporary Christians

John THE BAPTIST, SINCE THE TIME OF THE Counter-Reformation, has been lost to the Christian tradition. Some biblical scholars try to confine him to the status of an Old Testament figure. With the decline of monasticism, his severe virtues seem irrelevant to many modern Christians. It is one of the aims of this book to make one, small attempt to restore John to the beadroll of Christian heroes, to reinstate him to his proper and august role, as he is depicted in the ancient renditions of the Deësis, as an intercessor for all humankind second only to Mary. John has much to offer as a model for contemporary Christians, as we would expect of the saint who received from Christ's own lips the incomparable accolade: "among those born of women no one has arisen greater than John the Baptist" (Matthew 11:11).

There is a psychological block that has grown up over centuries between modern man and sanctity. The ex-monk, Martin Luther, in the sixteenth century denigrated the virtues of monastic life and set in motion a disdain for ascetic virtues like fasting and self-denial. This has led to a twenty-first-century fascination with a user-friendly religion that never talks of sin or judgment or hell. Many modern churches have no crosses and feature a theatre-style architecture with rock-religion festivals for large congregations. The mediocrity of much spirituality today is that it is too superficial, too lacking in intellectual substance, and not steeped in the Scriptures, which are the Word of God, especially any word of contradiction to the value system of the culture. Simone Weil once said, "Our age is in need of a sanctity that has genius." Saint John the Baptist can provide for us the model of a sanctity that has genius.

John's call to holiness emphasizes the sterner Christian virtues that need reinvigoration today. We can't form an ideal of holiness until we have an idea of sin. Only sixty years ago whole Catholic families would go to confession every Saturday afternoon. Today, this practice has disappeared. Is this because we no longer need forgiveness? Or because we don't sin any more? Such questions are deeply troubling. But these very attitudes may have been what led John to proclaim to his hearers the need for repentance and the imminence of the coming judgment and the advent of the kingdom of heaven. John preached a very basic (not mystical) spirituality in which the first essential is repentance: "Who warned you to flee from the wrath to come? Bear fruit worthy of repentance"

(Matthew 3:7–8). John's repentance is first, a turning away from sin, though it is not confined to this. The first step requires the recognition of our sins and the sorrow for their great harm. The unbridgeable chasm between the divine and the human can only be crossed by repentance, for that is the basis for us to live again in God's love. The second requirement is the performance of good works. Remember the lines from Josephus, *Antiquities of the Jews*: "In his view this was a necessary preliminary if baptism was to be acceptable to God. They must not employ it to gain pardon for whatever sins they committed, but as a consecration of the body implying that the soul was already thoroughly cleansed by right behaviour."[1] John did not find words of repentance adequate, he insisted that repentance first be expressed in action, "the fruits of repentance." He would tolerate no complacency or presumption that wished to rely for salvation on descent from Abraham. John was preparing a new people for the Lord, and he wanted each person to be judged on his own merits and actions.

This repentance of John's is presented, like the prophets of old, in a context of impending crisis—the wrath of God and the coming of judgment with its prospect of unquenchable fire. John was not one to mince words, but to those who backed up their sincere repentance with good deeds, John offered what Mark describes as "a baptism of repentance for the forgiveness of sins" (Mark 1:4). If John were alive today, his priority, it would seem, would be a restoration of the sacrament of confession to a position of central importance. He would require sincere acts of mortification as evidence of good faith. And he would point out to us that in this *metanoia*, or conversion, we are receiving a surgical removal of the roots of sin that can only be achieved in this way. And he would insist that repentance is an act that can never be finished. It must become a constant state of the soul, if we are to flee the wrath that is to come. It is not enough to sin no more, it is necessary to continue doing good works, to share our riches with the poor.

The key to John's spirituality lies in understanding the insistence of the fathers that John's monasticism is not just a model for monks, but for all the faithful. This is the same notion as that of Saint Tikhon of Zadonsk, a saint of the Eastern Orthodox tradition, who held that each and every Christian can and must become "an untonsured monk." Saint John the Baptist's spirituality is an example of what Paul Evdokimov in his *Ages of the Spiritual Life* calls "interiorized monasticism."[2] John's virtues can be adapted to provide a monasticism for all, because John was such a strong advocate of the basics in Christian life. We should not be startled by this idea that we should all become monks. It does not mean that we must take vows of poverty, chastity and obedience, but it does mean that, in the spirit of the Beatitudes, we should become poor in spirit, pure of heart and obedient to the will of God.

In the Gospels we see that John is a pioneer in the acts of prayer, fasting and almsgiving, the three great lenten virtues. When the disciples come upon Our Lord praying, one of them asks, "Lord, teach us to pray, as John taught his disciples" (Luke 11:1). John is the first great teacher of prayer we encounter in the

PRphet

New Testament. From his stay in the desert, he knew the therapeutic effects of silence, solitude and contemplation. Jesus, like John, would always seek a lonely place to pray. That teacher of John in the desert, the Holy Spirit, does not speak to us over the din of crowds or television. He whispers to us as gently as the flutter of the wings of a dove. Prayer requires great effort and a strong resistance to laziness and distraction. While we do not have any of John's prayers, we do know that when Jesus was asked to teach his disciples to pray as John did, he taught them the Our Father. We might surmise from this that the essence of John's prayer was to get his disciples to conform themselves totally to the will of God and in the simplest possible words. Regular prayer or the habit of praying without ceasing is the best means for cultivating the ability to walk in another's shoes, to see the world through God's eyes, to acquire that humility which is the foundation of a spiritual life.

On another occasion in Matthew's Gospel, the disciples of John come to Jesus and ask, "Why do we and the Pharisees fast often, but your disciples do not fast?" Jesus replies that, "when the bridegroom is taken away from them…then they will fast" (Matthew 9:14–15). Unfortunately, we do not today think of fasting as necessary, as John and Jesus and Judaism and the early church did. In the early church, it was common to observe a fast two days a week, Wednesday and Friday. Fasting is a sign of our detachment from the things of earth and an acknowledgment that we are abiding by the Lord's command to fast until the Bridegroom returns. It is, therefore, concrete evidence of our expectation of the Parousia. The power of fasting can be seen in the book of

Jonah where, to Jonah's chagrin, both the people and the animals of Nineveh put on sackcloth and fast, and God relents from destroying Nineveh. This power of fasting can also be seen in Jesus' comment that some devils can be cast out only by prayer and fasting (Mark 9:29). Have we disregarded the Lord's command to fast? Have we missed out on the opportunities fasting offers us? Fasting is the body's participation in the training of the soul. It leads to a freedom of heart and mind and an independence from material things. John's thirty years of fasting in the desert is memorialized for us in Rodin's statue of the ascetic John. Jesus has left us the example of fasting during his forty days and forty nights in the desert. Fasting has a special consequence of putting spiritual and material things into a proper perspective. It is a sign of our solidarity with the poor. It is much to be hoped that our bishops will realize that in making fasting optional, both in much of Lent and before receiving the Eucharist, they have, as Eamon Duffy has argued, abandoned the focus of Catholic identity, a communal practice as old as the church itself and a command of the Lord's that cannot simply be made a matter of private choice without incalculable losses. There is no substitute for fasting. Fasting and prayer are the twin pillars of spiritual life. Fasting is the way in which the body participates in our prayer. As John, the emaciated ascetic, would surely counsel us, we neglect the practice of fasting at the peril of our souls.

The third Lenten virtue, almsgiving, is one John recommended to the crowds that asked him, "What, then, should we do?" In reply he said to them, "Whoever has two coats must share with anyone who has none; and whoever has food must do likewise" (Luke 3:10–11). In the small samples we get in the Gospels of John's preaching, these verses stand out as his urgent concern for the poorest of the poor. John recommends almsgiving not just to benefit the poor, the direct beneficiaries, but to benefit the givers also. This advice is given in the context of preparing the way of the Lord and of establishing with eschatological urgency that "every tree therefore that does not bear good fruit is cut down and thrown into the fire" (Luke 3:9). John is always focused on the test of deeds. He is saying to us that it is not by what you say but by what you do that you will be judged. John would be a great exponent of the examen, the daily examination of conscience to test whether our actions have matched our words, whether our practice of virtue has matched our ambitions. It is the only way that one can distinguish the good tree from the bad tree—by its fruits.

We have noted that in the desert John was the first to practice, what have become in imitation of him, the monastic and Christian virtues of poverty, chastity and obedience. The essence of the ascetic, as the etymology of the word tells us, is exercise, spiritual exercise designed to teach us love. John taught us these virtues more by example than by precept. His father was a priest and probably well-off economically. True poverty is not necessarily to lack material goods, but to be detached from them, to give up voluntarily their dominion over us. But John did both. He left his father's house probably around the age of twelve and practiced the most severe poverty known to man—a practice without precedence in Jewish culture except among some of the prophets, most notably Elijah. Riches in that culture were a sign of God's blessing, as we see in the case of Job. So John was very clearly establishing this countercultural virtue of poverty as a new Christian ideal.

In somewhat the same fashion, John was unmarried and cultivated chastity in a culture where each man was expected to marry. John and Jesus were exceptions to the pattern in their society. So far as we know, most of the apostles, including Peter, were married. When did this virtue of chastity, of purity of heart, first became a Christian virtue? It was, I believe, in the Judean desert, where John went to purify himself in the burning sands, to live like an angel and to give his whole heart to the Lord. For as Saint Paul has taught us, chastity without charity is a meaningless virtue. John was cleansing himself of all distractions in order to concentrate on the Lord. He was teaching us the same lesson as that old song, "I have no use for divided hearts: I give mine whole and not in parts."

The older we get, the harder it is to regard obedience as a virtue. It is annoying and constraining to be subject always to the will of another. But in his desert school, taught by the Holy Spirit, John learned his lessons slowly. First he learned that always to obey is to be a martyr without dying. Second and only over a long period, did he come to realize the lesson that Dante has taught us: "In your will, O Lord, is our peace." For this lesson comes home to us only through the slow progress of self-denial and the cultivation of that humility which can say and mean: "He must increase, but I must decrease." Fidelity to God in temptation and in struggle is impossible except for those who have led a harsh and austere life of detachment. And John's life was a succession of detachments—

from his home, from his clothing, from his pride and his selfishness, and in his imprisonment, from his freedom, from his role as precursor, and finally from his head. While we—weak humans without John's angelic virtues—cannot imitate John in all his detachments, we can imitate him in his immense journey to the interior of the soul by imitating his virtues of poverty, chastity and obedience in our own adapted ways. We should remember that for John, his death to the world in the desert did not mean a refusal to live in the world, for John sent his disciples back from the desert to do just that. He never set up a monastery in the desert like the Essenes. His headquarters were the desert, but from there, he traveled along the Jordan River to baptize and to preach and to teach. We should recall that the tax collectors addressed John as a rabbi and teacher when they said, "Teacher, what should we do?" (Luke 3:12). We too are his students who desire to ask him, "Teacher, how do we advance in the spiritual life?"

When John puts off the old man in the desert, behold the new has come! John becomes our personal precursor to Christ, our guide to Christ. His innovative dedication to baptism should be a reminder to us of our own baptism in Christ, for as Paul tells us, "Therefore we have been buried with him by baptism into death, so that, just as Christ was raised from the dead by the glory of the Father, so we too might walk in newness of life" (Romans 6:4). This reflection on our own baptism is a revelation of the divinity of Christ and of our inclusion into his body, as we await a resurrection like his. There is an ancient and lovely inscription on the Johannine Baptistery of the Lateran Basilica that reads: "Sinner, go down into the sacred fountain that your sins may be washed away. You go down old in sin, you come up in the newness of youth."

As we heard from the fathers, the ministries of grace are not given for just one age; they are permanent, and John's role as precursor and guide to Christ is his permanent role in Christianity. In the fourth Gospel, John the witness gives us his own distinctive Christology. He is for us, as he was for Jesus' contemporaries, a witness to the light of the world so that he might bring all to believe in this light. He is the first to testify that Jesus is "the Lamb of God who takes away the sin of the world" (John 1:29). Jesus becomes for us the scapegoat of Leviticus 16:20–22 that bears all the sins of the people and is exiled into the wilderness. He also becomes the Passover Lamb, who is sacrificed to procure our freedom. John's faith response is to emphasize his personal experience of Christ: "I myself have seen and have testified that this is the Son of God." It is because of this personal experience that John is able to say, "I am not worthy to untie the thong of his sandal" (John 1:27). We too must cultivate this deep sense of the presence of God, for to live in the presence of God is to begin the journey on the long road to sanctity.

John would have us come so close to Christ that he is our friend, as John was "the friend of the bridegroom, who stands and hears him" (John 3:29). John's dedication to Christ should lead us to hear him, for in imitating Christ, we form the habits that advance us in the pursuit of holiness. One of those habits and one of the ways of hearing Christ, a way that John pursued in the desert, was reading the Scriptures. John often quotes the prophets, especially Isaiah and Malachi and his imagery, like Lamb of God and Light of the World, and his apocalyptic images of fire, the winnowing fork and the chaff, all come from his deep reading in Scripture, his Scripture, which was the Old Testament.

The spirituality of John, like the spirituality of the medieval monks, was shaped by the reading of Scripture, *lectio divina*, a phrase more accurately translated as praying the Scriptures. As the Word of God has been restored by Vatican II to a central place in the life of the church, it is time we restored the ancient practice of praying the Scriptures. Saint Jerome used to remind us that ignorance of Scripture is ignorance of Christ. As John knew, the Word of God comes from God and leads to God. It is the means by which we, like John, live in God. Christ himself practiced this prayerful reading of Scripture in the synagogue at Nazareth when he read in the scroll from the prophet Isaiah and then proclaimed, "Today this Scripture has been fulfilled in your hearing" (Luke 4:21). Just as John had the Holy Spirit as his private tutor in the desert, we too can have the Holy Spirit guide us to discern Christ in the Scriptures. The Holy Spirit inspired the Scriptures, and he who breathed in also breathes out. The Spirit leads us to see that the Scriptures are the nourishment for the mind, just as the Eucharist is nourishment for the body and soul. Thus, we must always remember that praying the Scriptures is different from reading the Scriptures. Scripture is the science of salvation, and we must not read it like spectators, but pray it like participants. *Lectio divina* is a dialogue and we must have the patience to wait for the Holy Spirit to speak to us.

Like the crowds at the river Jordan, we come to John and say, "What are we to do?" John was the road maker, the trailblazer who prepared the way for Christ, and in doing so, he also prepared his disciples, patiently molding them into spokesmen for God and servants of the Word. As he sensed the imminence of his own death, he passed his disciples over to Christ. In John's Gospel the last words we hear from John are when he leads Andrew and probably Philip to Jesus, saying, "Look, here is the Lamb of God!" and from there they become Apostles of Christ. This is what John would do for us: send us to Christ to become his apostles and, like John himself, missionaries to the world. Teachers are common, but masters are rare, and John is a rare master of the spiritual life. He wishes to teach us to give away the gift that has been given to us—faith. To do so, we must have the same fire and zeal and spirit as John. We must be friends to sinners but fearful enemies of figures who create public scandal. We must pursue perfection and as Augustine assured us, we have no better model of perfection than John. He teaches us that the messenger of God must be austere and mortified, if his words are to be heard and accepted and able to pierce the most hardened hearts. If we have not converted someone to Christ, what shall we have to say at the particular judgment? And if we do, we shall have that reward of joy that John speaks of when he says that "The friend of the bridegroom, who stands and hears him, rejoices greatly at the bridegroom's voice. For this reason my joy has been fulfilled" (John 3:29). And it is this joy which is the echo of Christ's life in us. Saint Augustine once remarked that "The voice [of John the Baptist] gradually ceases its office in the measure that the soul progresses toward Christ." "He must increase, I must decrease." Saint John Chrysostom was fond of comparing John to a bridge: "He spans the reality of today and stretches off into the future."[3] He is the permanent precursor and guide to Christ, and it is to him that we owe it that we are Christians. He is the universal missionary, the voice crying out to all peoples. He is the one who can give us a renewed sense of sin and restore to its proper place the sacrament of reconciliation. He can restore fasting as the indelible badge of Catholics. He can remind the entire church that it is an apocalyptic community awaiting the return of the Christ at the Parousia. As we live in the most consumption-minded culture in history, who could better teach us the practice of poverty and of simplicity of life? Do we not have an urgent need for John's virtues today as a source both of courage and of spiritual renewal?

## QUESTIONS FOR REFLECTION

- What obstacles does modern culture place in the way of a proper appreciation of John the Baptist and his rigorous form of spirituality?

- Why is repentance the first priority in John's spirituality? What role do actions play in John's version of repentance? Why would it be a reasonable assumption to maintain that John would wish to restore the sacrament of confession to a position of central importance in Christian spirituality?

- John's spirituality would require each of us to be untonsured monks, to observe poverty, chastity and obedience in the world and to practice our own versions of prayer, fasting and almsgiving. How feasible is such a program? With John and the Holy Spirit as our tutors, what can we not accomplish?

- Describe what John's relationship was with Christ and what he would like ours to be. What role could *lectio divina*, or praying the Scriptures, play in achieving this relationship with Christ?

**NOTES**
[1] Josephus, *Antiquities of the Jews*, XVIII–XX, p. 83.
[2] Paul Evdokimov, *Ages of the Spiritual Life*, (Crestwood, N.Y.: St. Vladimir's Seminary Press, 1998), p. 9.
[3] Quoted in Rétif, p. 12.

# A Spirituality Appendix: Devotions to John the Baptist

Considering the prominent position of John the Baptist in the Gospels and church history, it is surprising that there are so few prayers to John the Baptist or devotions in his honor. For this appendix, I have composed a Litany to John the Baptist, as I could find none available, and I have also included a few notable prayers or reflections from Christian tradition.

## A Litany to Saint John the Baptist

The word *litany* derives from a Greek word for "plea" or "entreaty" and denotes a prayer of supplication. Litanies were once part of the celebration of the Eucharist and were incorporated into the office of daily prayer. They seem to have originated in Antioch in the fourth century. Known in the eastern churches as "petitions," they were transmitted throughout the East and to the West after their adoption by the church at Constantinople. Their pattern of fixed petitions and short responses led them to be recited and often sung in Christian churches and monasteries throughout the world.

Lord, have mercy on us.

*Christ, have mercy on us.*

Lord, have mercy on us.

Christ, hear us.

*Christ, graciously hear us.*

God, the Father of heaven, *have mercy on us.*

God, the Son, redeemer of the world, *have mercy on us.*

Holy Trinity, one God, *have mercy on us.*

Holy Mary, *pray for us.*

Saint John the Baptist, *pray for us.*

Cousin of the Lord,

Greeter of the savior from your mother's womb,

Patron of the unborn,

First Christian saint of the desert,

Precursor of the Messiah,

Despiser of the comforts of earth,

Exemplar of humility,

Taught by the Holy Spirit,

Lover of silence,

Lover of solitude,

Model of monks and hermits,

Apostle of the forgetfulness of self,

Herald of Christ,

First of Christians,

First of evangelists,

Bridge of the testaments,

Gateway to the Gospels,

Mediator of things old and new,

Preacher of repentance,

Prophet of the Most High,

Prophet and more than a prophet,

Elijah of Christ,

Crown of prophecy,

Culmination of the prophets,

Shining lamp of the light of the world,

Trumpet of heaven,

Minister of grace,

Baptizer of Christ,

Chosen messenger of the Father,

Vehicle of the Holy Spirit,

Friend of the Bridegroom,

First witness of the Trinity,

Most excellent of the human race,

Critic of tyrants,

Defender of the marriage bond,

Master of the science of prayer,

Preparer of the way to Christ,

Advocate of the excluded,

Friend of the poor,

Scourge of the unfaithful and the unrepentant,

Hero of God,

Betrayed by a dancer,

Martyr for the truth,

Boundary marker of the epochs,

Forerunner of both the first and second coming of Christ,

In the waters of the Jordan, your Son, O God, was baptized by John and anointed with the Spirit. *Lord, save your people.*

By John's preaching of repentance and reconciliation, *Lord, save your people.*

By John's example of desert spirituality, *Lord, save your people.*

By your gift of the fullness of the Holy Spirit to your Precursor, *Lord, save your people.*

Lamb of God, who takes away the sins of the world, *spare us, O Lord.*

Lamb of God, who takes away the sins of the world, *graciously hear us, O Lord.*

Lamb of God, who takes away the sins of the world, *have mercy on us.*

God made him the Precursor of the Messiah

*And the prophet of the Most High.*

Let us pray: God, our Father, the voice of John the Baptist challenges us to repentance and points the way to Christ the Lord. Open our ears to hear his message, and free our hearts to turn from our sins and receive the life of the Gospel. We ask this through Christ our Lord. Amen.[1]

Saint Anselm (1033–1109) has left us the following touching prayer of repentance to John in his *Prayers and Meditations*.[2]

### PRAYER TO SAINT JOHN THE BAPTIST

St John:

you are that John who baptized God;

you were praised by an archangel

before you were begotten by your father;

you were full of God

before you were born of your mother;

you knew God before you knew the world;

you showed your mother the mother bearing God

before the mother who bore you within her

showed you the day.

It was of you that God said:

"Among them that are born of women

there has not risen a greater".

To you, sir, who are so great, holy and blessed,

comes a guilty, creeping thing,

a wretched little man

whose senses are almost dead with grief,

and, what grieves him even more, a sinner with a dead soul.

To you, so great a friend of God,

he comes, very fearful, doubtful of his salvation,

because he is sure of the greatness of his guilt,

but hoping in your greater grace;

for your grace, sir, is greater than my guilt;

what you are able to do before God

will more than blot out all my wickedness.

To you, then, sir,

whom grace has made such a friend of God,

to you, in my distress, I flee.

I, the accused of God through manifold iniquities,

worth nothing because of so much misery,

come to you whom grace has filled with blessedness.

Truly, sir, I admit this:

my sins have made me what I am,

but you have not made yourself what you are,

but the grace of God with you.

So remember, sir,

that as the grace of God made you so high,

so your mercy can raise him up

who is laid so low by his guilt.

Alas, what have I made of myself?

What was I, O God, as you had made me—

and how have I made myself again!

In sin I was conceived and born,

but you washed me and sanctified me;

and I have defiled myself still more.

Then I was born in sin of necessity,

but now I wallow in it of my own free will.

In sin I was conceived in ignorance,

but these sins I commit willingly, readily, and openly.

From them in mercy I was led forth by you;

to these miseries I have led myself.

I was redeemed from them by goodness,

and I have broken with that redemption by wickedness.

You healed, good God, a soul wounded in its first parents;

    I, wicked man, have killed what was healed.

You set aside, merciful Lord, the old rags of original sin,

    and clothed me in the garments of innocence,

    promising me incorruptibility in the future;

    and casting off what you had given me,

    I busied myself with sordid sins;

    despising what you had promised,

I chose rather the sorrows of eternal misery.

You had made the son of your wrath

    into the son of your grace,

    and I, contemptuous of that,

    made myself the son of your hatred.

You refashioned your gracious image in me,

And I superimposed upon it the image that is hateful.

    Alas, alas, how could I?

How could I, miserable and crazy little man that I am,

    how could I superimpose that image

        upon the image of God?

. . .

Then, by the great merit of your Baptizer,

    renew in me the grace of your baptizing.

Go before me with your grace; follow me with your mercy.

Give me back through the sorrow of penitence

what you had given through the sacrament of baptism.
Give to me who asks,

    what you gave to him who knew you not.

Refashion the face that I have spoiled,

    restore the innocence that I have violated.

You, Lord, were not involved in that sin

    which you were born to bear.

Lord, take away the sin that I have contracted in living.

Take away, you who take away the sin of the world,

    these which are sins of the world,

    which I carry from living in the world.

Take away, you who take away the sin of the world,

by the merits of him who with that same word of witness

    pointed you out to the world,

take away the sins that I have contracted in the world;

    take from me whatever is not from you,

for I hate whatever is from me; and I still hope in you.

And you, St John,

    who showed to the world

    him who takes away the sin of the world,

    by the grace given to you

gain for me that mercy to take away my sins.

. . .

Jesus, good Lord,

    if you perform the work that he testifies of you,

John, revealer of God, if you witness to what he performs,

    be it to me according to your word.

Lord, from whom comes healing, heal me.

Do this for me, Lord, since you are able to do it,

    you are the great Lord,

and you, John, are "great in the sight of the Lord."

You can do all things by your own nature;

    you are very powerful before him.

You are the high and good God,

    and you are the very good friend

of him who is in eternity the merciful and blessed God.

                      Amen.

**NOTES**

[1] This last paragraph is from the Mass of the Birth of John the Baptist, June 24. Many of the titles have been culled from the writings of fathers and doctors of the church.

[2] *The Prayers and Meditations of St Anselm, with the Proslogion*, Sister Benedicta Ward, S.L.G., trans. and intro. (New York: Penguin, 1973), pp. 127–134.

# Index